BROKEN

A True Story of Spiritual Abuse

CLAIRE LARSEN

WESTBOW
PRESS®
A DIVISION OF THOMAS NELSON
& ZONDERVAN

WestBow Press books may be ordered through
booksellers or by contacting:

WestBow Press
A Division of Thomas Nelson & Zondervan
1663 Liberty Drive
Bloomington, IN 47403
www.westbowpress.com
844-714-3454

Scripture quotations taken from The Holy Bible, New International
Version® NIV® Copyright © 1973 1978 1984 2011 by Biblica,
Inc. TM. Used by permission. All rights reserved worldwide.

ISBN: 978-1-6642-9371-7 (sc)
ISBN: 978-1-6642-9372-4 (e)

Library of Congress Control Number: 2023903738

Print information available on the last page.

WestBow Press rev. date: 03/07/2023

This book is dedicated to those who remain "in Christ" still today. Mercy, grace, and peace be yours from God our Father and our Lord and Savior Jesus Christ.

CONTENTS

INTRODUCTION

Dear Reader,

This work is my labor of love for the body of Christ, God's chosen and dearly loved sons and daughters. These pages contain my tragic story of spiritual abuse within Christian organizations. I desire the opportunity to have a voice regarding what happened and, in my own words, tell the story from my perspective.

There are many times in the past several years I've felt as if I haven't been allowed to share my thoughts or opinions, or my requested needs and desires have been brushed aside. I've debated whether or not to tell my story many times. Ultimately, this feeling of being silenced for so long has provoked me to make the decision that it's finally time to speak. I determined to write my story.

As you read, you may be surprised by the stark contrast within the content. Just as Christ came into the earth and had boundless compassion for the broken yet stern rebuke for the pious, religious leaders of his day, this book will be in much of the same manner. You may be surprised to hear these two opposite extremes presented within these pages, but take heart. Jesus spoke in this same way when he walked the earth, encountering both the broken and boastful as well.

My story may very well represent others who have answered the call into missions or ministry, only to encounter a horrendous 'system' within the Church itself and its organizations. This 'system,' as I call it, is a stumbling block for many and prevents people from carrying the gospel to the unreached. I don't know who or how many I'm speaking for, but I know you're out there too.

Recently, we met a missionary couple who faced problems with their agency during their family's first field experience, and the husband stated it had taken him *three years* to recover. Some friends of ours knew another missionary couple who experienced similar problems within their agency. I read one young woman's blog about her experience and was saddened to see she had *left the faith* altogether. These are just three of countless examples kept hidden from the masses.

If you are reading this book and have suffered abuse from 'the system' described in these pages, can I just say: *I'm so sorry.* I'm sorry this happened to you. It should never have been this way, and it shouldn't be this way. It grieves the heart of God. He has seen and has not abandoned nor forgotten you.

On the flip side, I want to bring to attention the danger of wolves in sheep's clothing within the body of Christ. My desire is to inform, educate, and equip believers to identify how some of these men and women operate in order to recognize, prevent, or deal with these tactics. My desire is for the Church to stand up and call these men to account, and if these men and women refuse, to suffer ejection from the body (Matthew 18:17). One must exhibit true faith in Christ through their deeds. "By their fruit you will recognize them" (Matthew 7:16).

> "Dear friends, although I was very eager to write to you about the salvation we share, I felt I had to write and urge you to contend for the faith that was once for all entrusted to the saints. For certain men whose condemnation was written about long ago have secretly slipped in among you. They are godless men, who change the grace of our God into a license for immorality and deny Jesus Christ our only Sovereign and Lord." Jude 3-4

While not all church leaders are "wolves," the latter section of this book explores areas in the general population of American Christian church leadership today that quite possibly needs rearrangement or revamping. I have held up to the light of the Word various aspects of the modern-day Church, considering and comparing its current operational status with God's standards and heart for the world. The results I've concluded are potentially controversial however necessary for reconsideration.

I claim no title nor office in the Church but only servant of the Lord and member of his kingdom of priests. I've never attended seminary nor do I adhere to any particular denomination as I believe each one has its faults. I claim no talent or wisdom but only share my thoughts based upon my experience and observations of the Church in light of Scripture. I admit I'm not perfect, and I know I have many of my own weaknesses. After reading my story, you'll have a better understanding of how one can feel weak. However, I do know one thing and that is this: Jesus Christ and him crucified (1 Corinthians 2:2).

If my life's contribution to the world is simply to share my story with the hope of raising awareness and guiding the Church and its existence toward a better end result, then I willingly share it for Jesus and his Bride. I hope this book's message speaks loudly and clearly because I believe through it, the Lord may have something to say.

It's always worth hearing the Lord speak. Pray and ask the Holy Spirit if the words I share could be the thoughts and words of God or not (1 Peter 4:11). As such, I believe God may be speaking to us today:

It's time to clean and organize my house!

★All names have been changed and locations remain vague in order to respect privacy and protect security.

CHAPTER 1
THE CALL

In 2013 my husband Chad and I felt the Lord calling us to adopt. We pursued his heart for orphans for over four years, attempting to adopt a sibling group from Ethiopia. Just when we were about to receive our "match," they closed their doors to international adoption. Sadly, this process ended with our dossier on a desk somewhere in their country.

Shortly afterward, we followed the Lord on a worship team short-term mission trip (STMT) to Haiti with our church in August 2017, and it rocked our world. We still had a heart for orphans and learned a few things about a Haitian orphanage through one of the founders of the Christian mission in which we were serving. We were greatly challenged by the poverty and, despite their humble circumstances, their joyful worship of God.

When we returned home, we met with our global outreach director Jerry, expressing our interest in orphan care. He proposed we become the church's main advocate for our four global partners' child sponsorship programs. He invited us to travel with him to Asia on the next

STMT. We agreed and prepared to join a medical team in order to speak with the national pastor Patrick and his American wife Heidi about their child sponsorship program.

Several months later we arrived in Asia on the STMT and met with our church's national partners, Patrick and Heidi. We quickly found out their child sponsorship program had dissolved for various reasons. However, they had purchased a music academy three years prior for a "business as mission" (BAM) project in order to share the gospel with the patrons and help bring an income for their church planting efforts. Chad and I both have music educator backgrounds, so we thought this might be the Lord leading us into international missions. Jerry was very encouraging to us while we were there, telling us he saw something special in the way in which we were serving.

Let me back up here just a bit and tell you what had been happening in my personal and spiritual life. Near the end of our adoption process, I started a home-based business selling skincare. I was 'all in' and so excited to have something of my own after years of being a stay-at-home mom. The older two were in school, and I just had a new baby.

I had a lot of fun selling products, pleasing customers, and dreaming of what it could become. In my mind, it had the potential to provide our family with financial freedom so I could bring my husband home to me and away from the high school band director position that had taken his time, focus, and energy for twelve years with little left over for me and the kids. All my hopes and dreams were wrapped up in this thing: financial freedom, legacy, vanity, belonging, team, purpose, vision, you name it.

What started as fun business "side gig" eventually turned into an all-consuming burden I couldn't bear as friends and family turned me down for two years. I took the rejection personally and just about imploded. It was about this time that I read the book *When I Lay My Isaac Down* by Carol Kent. I was challenged to take the thing that I loved most and sacrifice it on the altar, believing God had better plans for my life than I could come up with myself.

Even though I had been a Christian my whole life, the intense grief associated with overwhelming rejection and a business failure stirred up many past griefs—'losing' my husband to his job, feeling rejected as a vocalist in college, two miscarriages, and an adoption process that never materialized—drove me to the Lord's feet. The culmination of grief was overwhelming. I rededicated my life to be used for his glory if he could use anything at all. God took me from being an ambassador for the skincare company to being His kingdom ambassador.

After we returned home from that STMT to Asia, I made the final decision to quit the business and was driven by the shame of failure and rejection into a time hidden with the Lord. During this time, I dove into the Word and my eyes were opened. I repented of my focus on things that took me away from him such as my pursuit of money as my saving grace and path to freedom. I didn't realize that this thing had become my idol. It had stolen my attention and devotion away from the Lord.

Chad and I spent several months praying and seeking

the Lord regarding the opportunity to serve as missionaries in Asia through this particular BAM project. I knew something this radical needed serious confirmation, or I wasn't going to go. God confirmed through Scripture, through various individuals' prophetic prayers, through dreams, through the Holy Spirit speaking to my spirit in the early morning hours, and even through one very personal, supernatural encounter with the Lord. Regardless of my own fears, doubts, and hesitations, I knew it was him.

The book *Passion for the Heart of God* by John Willis Zumwalt was also integral in pushing me towards a lost world and the call to spread the gospel. When God calls and stirs your heart to "go," it's an amazing thing to answer that call. With renewed enthusiasm and excitement to serve the Lord and participate in the Great Commission, we met with Jerry in his office to communicate our intentions. Soon after, we met online with national partners Patrick and Heidi to offer ourselves for the music academy project!

CHAPTER 2

PRE-FIELD

U pon their acceptance to their field team for this assignment, we submitted an application to the Agency of which they are members. One month later, we found ourselves across the country at our first Agency training session. Since Jerry had determined we should take the long-term missionary track, we were given an extensive list of requirements and college courses to accomplish during pre-field. I was absolutely overwhelmed. Much of the training was focused on church planting efforts, not necessarily tools for establishing and running a BAM to support the national partner's church planting efforts. We took what we could from these trainings.

During that week, we had several interviews. Following our final interview, we were commissioned at the annual conference. Jerry flew out from our home sending church to represent us.

When we returned home, we had a lot of support raising and studies to accomplish. We hosted many families for dinner to share the project's vision and visited five other churches in our area. Not one of these churches made any commitment for monthly support. I was exhausted and disheartened by the time and preparation with so little response.

Sometime during our pre-field, we were invited by and transitioned over to a smaller side-branch of our Agency. This branch was intended for missionaries partnering with an existing national partner, typically in "creative access" (Christian-hostile) countries in the East. We agreed and transitioned over to this side of the Agency, thinking it had long been established with a successful track record. What we didn't know was the main leader was retiring and bringing on two new executive directors (ED's) into the home office to continue building this smaller organization, "piggy-backing" on the larger, established organization.

Around this time, Jerry and his wife Janet had us over for burgers and announced he would also be transitioning from global outreach director at our home sending church to this Agency, and his wife would be joining as well. We were excited by the news! At least we wouldn't be alone in this endeavor!

Our homework assignments began to change because we were this Agency branch's first "guinea pig" family. Jerry and the two ED's began navigating new policies and procedures. We felt caught between the education department's long list of assignments given to us at our first training and the new side-branch's cancellation and alteration of what was actually required. It was very confusing. At least the burden of taking four different seminary courses was lifted off my shoulders!

In between all of this, I was really enjoying this season of drawing close to Jesus during my time at home. Worship music would be on for hours. I would dance and sing, encountering afresh the unbridled, unconditional love of Jesus. I began to sense his Presence and spent time listening and journaling what I believed the Lord was saying to me. Bible reading was exciting and regular, and I was hearing short phrases in my spirit as I was waking up in the early morning hours. I had never had a relationship with God like this before, and I was enthralled and eager for more!

I wanted so badly to find out what my spiritual gift was and find a place of true belonging in the Church. Because I was so passionate about worship and loved singing, I tried leading a couple songs on the women's worship team at Tuesday morning Bible study. When I wasn't asked to lead worship again after those few songs, I felt the bitter sting of rejection.

Weeks later, I was finally brave enough to bring it up in conversation with a close friend on worship team. She told me, "You don't have a professional voice." I nodded in agreement, trying to make my heart digest this information too. After that, it didn't take long for me to step down all together from three years of women's worship team, serving on djembe or vocal harmonies. I lost my voice as my hopes were dashed and a piece of my heart got crushed.

Continuing pre-field, Chad and I managed to lead a STMT to Asia with four other church members during spring break. We did all the normal serving activities that we had done the year before. This time, however, I recall Heidi was largely absent that week.

On the previous STMT trip with Jerry, we'd stop by Heidi's home for lunch and tea, relaxing in their place for a while before the next scheduled event for the day. This time, we were left sitting on the hard church stage. Then, if we were hungry, we'd have to go out into the busy city to find food with a church staff member. There was no midday rest. The heat alone was sweltering.

Heidi also hadn't provided dinner in her home, whereas, she previously had dinner ready for the visiting team at the end of a long day of activities. Multiple evenings, our team—hungry and physically spent—was falling asleep on their couch by the time fast food arrived an hour later. It was a stark contrast.

That summer, our family traveled cross-country again for another summer of trainings and conferences. Our older two kids were able to participate in a wonderful training for missionary children. Regardless of whether or not Chad and my training directly applied to the BAM project, we were happy the kids had something. Micah (one of the new ED's) and his wife joined us for the week-long training as they had just moved into town to work in the home office, so we were able to get to know them a little.

Finally, after eighteen months of completing assignments, reading books, sharing with friends and family, visiting churches and small groups, and support raising, our family was commissioned by our home church. Micah flew over for this special commencement. With Jerry standing right beside me like a proud spiritual father, I sensed I was laying down my life as a sacrifice for the cause of Christ (something many missionaries feel at their commissioning services, I imagine). I remember shaking and crying that morning on stage knowing I was being "sent out" from this body—my Church family of twelve years—into uncharted territory and an assignment I, knowingly, would have never accepted.

The next day, Chad and I flew to Asia with Jerry to locate an apartment, order a vehicle, and open a bank account. We stayed in Patrick's home for two weeks while we searched, selected, and signed a two-year lease with a landlord. We ordered some basic furnishings for the flat so when our whole family arrived, there would already be a place for us to land.

During the first week of the pre-trip, Jerry also led a meeting between us and Patrick and Heidi, outlining our expectations for the first year. They gave us two pages of expectations, with only *one* pertaining to Patrick and Heidi as they were to help us orient and acclimate. We weren't aware this was to become an issue as we were brand-new, inexperienced missionaries. Their expectation was in bold type on page two: **Start with weekly team meetings.**

After a seemingly successful pre-trip, Chad and I returned home and began sorting through all our things, filling our three-car garage with most of our belongings to sell. This alone was a gigantic task as every item we owned got touched. We sold our cars and everything else except personal belongings which we put inside a storage shed. We left basic furnishings in the house to be used as a rental since we planned to be gone for two years, if not more.

When it was time for our departure to the field, unfortunately, we ran across trouble with our Agency. Their medical director had just retired and a new one was in office. The new medical director didn't know the ropes and our Agency's new ED Micah also didn't foresee that we needed medical clearance. Consequently, our departure was delayed by several weeks as the hospital downloaded our entire lifespan of medical records onto a CD and snail mailed it across the country for some sort of approval.

While waiting for medical clearance from the Agency, our vehicle we flew halfway around the world to purchase had arrived on the lot in Asia and was promptly sold to someone else within a week because we weren't there to pick it up. Talk about frustrating!

At least Patrick was kind enough to send one of his staff to our apartment when our furniture arrived. Also, his American wife Heidi was kind enough to make the beds with the sheets we had brought over and put a few groceries in the fridge just before our family's arrival.

CHAPTER 3

ON THE FIELD

Our family finally arrived to our field on November 19, 2019. Heidi offered to get a few things for our home like hangars and helped set up the girl's closet. After that first week, however, her attention quickly dissipated.

It wasn't long before Patrick told us the music academy building had to relocate because city regulation no longer allowed business signs visible from the second floor in that area. In actuality, Patrick wanted a single building for all church and music academy activities combined rather than two separate locations.

Confused by the sudden change, we had no work space. The music academy building we knew was no longer going to be there. In addition, the building was filled with working church staff, their NGO (non-governmental organization) office, and a small bakery with its workers. There was nowhere for Chad to have an office. The music school was not currently functioning anyway, so we thought we'd just wait to start fresh with the new location.

Soon after our arrival, another couple from our Agency came to visit Patrick and Heidi. We had just met them a few months prior at the annual conference in the States. We didn't know they were in town until they had already left. I was very disappointed we hadn't been invited to meet with them. I was desperate for connection! They were from our own Agency!

Over the course of the first six weeks, we were expected to attend all meetings and special events amidst setting up our household and hosting our own Christmas caroling party for the church. I was overwhelmed by the combination of tasks at home paired with outside activities. We were busy learning how to perform basic functions in our new environment like figuring out what we could eat and obtaining groceries, getting around via various modes of transportation, and trying to communicate with people who spoke a foreign language. It was challenging and exasperating.

Our family traveled everywhere via Uber, except for a couple offers for rides from our field team leaders. They were engrossed in holiday activities and two STMT teams from the US. It was very, very busy. Congruently, we had a couple solid weeks of language lessons to undertake. Our children were overwhelmed by the culture change, struggling to eat the local flavors, combatting food allergy mishaps, and fighting sickness from the different germs in that country.

Due to the busyness of the field, Patrick and Heidi didn't have time for one-on-one connection with us. There was one short check-in during December late one evening after a Friday night small group. They didn't have time to help us secure another vehicle, give us any guidance on what it took to register as a foreigner, or find a different bank that actually allowed international transfers.

Following Christmas, the church staff took the week off. Things got quiet. Too quiet. We attended one birthday party that week.

Then Patrick and his family left the next week to visit where he grew up. After their return, *surely*, I thought, *they would reconnect with us and check how we were doing.* Nope. For the third week in a row, I was left alone in that fourteenth-floor apartment with my children. There was no one else on this team from our Agency. It was just us and them. I felt like I was alone on an island in the middle of an ocean—even though I was surrounded by a city of thirty-some million just outside my window. It was such a strange feeling.

During their absence, we stayed busy looking for other building options to suit both church and music academy multipurposed activities. We toured several buildings with one of the church staff and subsequently returned to our flat to draw up floor plans that could fit these different spaces. It was a lot of fun to create these drawings, envisioning what the building space could look like and how it would function.

At the end of three weeks apart, our family toured the same building options again with Patrick now that he was back from vacation. At the end of these tours, our family found ourselves headed to his two-story apartment to discuss what we'd seen. I texted Heidi on the way, offering to help order dinner since it was a last-minute decision of Patrick's for us to come over.

Our kids were so happy to see their two children again, and they all ran upstairs to play together. I was relieved. I had not seen our team for three weeks and had not received any check-ins or messages either. This meant our kids had also been without connection.

Chad and I sat down on their couch, and I was immediately comforted to be in a familiar space again. However, Heidi was very cold. Patrick asked her to come over and sit down for the meeting with us. She refused, and stayed in the kitchen cooking extra chicken for our family, apparently.

We began discussing the building search. Every time Patrick asked me a question, Heidi boisterously butted into the conversation from the kitchen, cutting off my ability to speak. Patrick even stopped her once and said he wanted to hear what I had to say. Heidi was very rude. She finally came over and sat down, and that's when they told us they were expecting their third child.

Patrick said his family was also working on plans to shift apartments. We had just finished settling into our apartment, but now everything else that we knew had plans for shifting: the pastor's home, the music building, and the church building. I felt so unstable as everything on the field seemed to be up in the air, yet we were the only thing settled. Although, we hadn't really even settled yet because there was no car, no working bank, no real "team," and a growing sense of alarm!

We also found out from Patrick that our stateside field team director Joe was trying to arrange a visit that month. Patrick had turned him down with the excuse that he was too busy to have him come. Patrick's decision to keep the field director from coming gave no consideration to our thoughts, needs, wants, or desires. Joe's visit and presence on the field at this crucial time wasn't just for Patrick, rather, it would have been beneficial for us. Ironically, in a few short days, Jerry and his wife Janet and their friends the Wilsons were due to visit the field and stay for the weekend.

It was time to eat. I got up from the couch and walked into the kitchen to dish our children's plates for dinner. That's when I saw it: Heidi's phone was lit up on the counter lying next to the serving area. I saw the most recent text she had sent to Patrick. "As long as it doesn't run up to dinner," regarding the meeting we'd just had and the dinner I was now dishing onto my kid's plates. My heart sank. I had been isolated in a foreign country for three weeks, finally trying to reconnect with our field team leaders, and she didn't even want us there. We stayed and ate dinner. We didn't eat much, and the extra chicken wasn't actually needed.

Right before we left, I asked Heidi if we could make a plan for the following weekend since we were to host Jerry, Janet, and the Wilsons. Her flippant response was, "Oh, we'll just hang out." My suggestion fell flat. I felt ignored. Our family left for the evening and took an Uber back to our flat.

Our first interaction after three weeks of no meaningful connection or supportive communication spoke volumes. The message came across loud and clear from Heidi: *Now that you're finally here and settled, I don't want you around and nothing you have to say is worth hearing.* I was crushed.

This behavior may be excusable if you're in your home country, but when you're a brand-new missionary on a foreign field, nothing feels familiar or safe. You literally feel like a helpless baby lying on the ground, flailing your arms and legs. You need to be picked up and held in a loving embrace. You desperately look for the hands that feed you and help you learn to walk in those early months. Anything less than nurturing, loving, and attentive care feels like sabotage from the ones who committed to bringing you onto their field in the first place.

The next day I texted Patrick and Heidi on our team thread, asking if we could at least come up with a meal plan while we had the two couples visiting. It wasn't long before Patrick sent a very detailed schedule for our visitors, filled with ministry events. I was surprised because Heidi had told me the very opposite! We finally did agree to a basic meal schedule, so I was able to make plans for cooking and hosting our guests at certain times.

A few days later, Jerry, Janet, and the Wilsons arrived. They spent the first evening over at Patrick and Heidi's flat. For some reason, we weren't invited. Then they messaged us that plans were changing, and they would be spending tomorrow's breakfast together too. We were not invited. I was completely distraught.

I had been feeling isolated and "dropped" by our field team leaders, and now our mentors were in town but not able to be with us for the first twenty-four hours? I had even adjusted the kids homeschool schedule to accommodate being with Jerry and Janet that Friday morning. I was dying inside.

Neither Chad nor I raised any issue with the sudden change of plans. I don't know why we didn't speak up, but I do know we were incredibly disoriented. We were also trusting our leaders to know what they were doing and didn't want to disrupt their plans or come against their wishes. We could have spoken up had we been able to think straight, but neither did they ask us what we needed or wanted.

While they met together the next morning, we busied ourself by going to the car dealership. Our Hindu neighbor had actually stepped in to help us purchase a vehicle (something that should have been immediately rectified by our field team leader Patrick the minute the first one was sold off). We had been taking Uber everywhere for two solid months which was very stressful and uncomfortable. Trying to work with the app, the payment, the drivers, the timing, and maneuvering and traveling around the bustling beehive of a city—while squished and sweaty in the back seat of those tiny cars with my three-year-old on my lap—had taken its toll on us.

We finally got to sit down in our apartment and share with Jerry and Janet our struggle with the lack of team meetings and our majorly disappointing time with Patrick and Heidi several nights before. Jerry and Janet's way of handling this unfortunate series of events was simply to say, "Oh, Claire, it's not you, it's Heidi."

Chad even requested Jerry to ask Patrick for regular team meetings, just like we had gone over three months before in our team expectations meeting led by Jerry. His response to Chad was, "*You* ask him." Jerry had acted as mediator in prior meetings between us and Patrick both in the States and on the field, so why couldn't he do this now when we asked for help?

That weekend, Janet, Mrs. Wilson, and I attended a bridal shower at Heidi's house. When we walked in the door, Heidi had just finished exuberantly greeting and warmly hugging one of their church attendees into her home. I walked in next and received no such welcome. I sat down next to Mrs. Wilson and made a side comment, "It sure would be nice to be greeted like that." Mrs. Wilson had witnessed the ensuing scene and agreed something was off-kilter.

Aside from these issues, the focus during Jerry, Janet, and the Wilson's visit was still on the music building search—one location in particular had piqued Patrick's interest. Chad had created a detailed, multi-page proposal for this building project, ultimately concluding it was too expensive. Never mind having a team meeting to discuss how we were doing, what we needed, or how they could help meet those needs! Never mind being treated with kindness, respect, and hospitality!

When all of us met together at our home the final evening, I had prepared a delicious stir fry meal (a welcome change from the local food). Next was tea and snacks. Finally, I ended the meal delighting our guests with a fancy tray of various ice cream bars for both adult and child alike. The kids secured their treats and scampered off to play in the girl's bedroom.

Internally, my mind was longing for our leaders to address the elephant in the room and work through the problems that had arisen within our team dynamics.

Sadly, no one said anything, and I was afraid to bring it up on such a lovely night for all six of our guests during the last meal of their stay. Soon, our well-fed guests began to pack for their airport departure.

Jerry and Janet gathered their belongings and emptied themselves from our guest bedroom. We gave hugs and they walked out the door with their suitcases, satisfied they had fulfilled their duty of supporting us by visiting the field. I'm not sure they realized they left us with unaddressed team issues or the fact they spent hours upon hours with Patrick and Heidi without us. Jerry had promised to play a game with our kids and didn't have time, yet he spent hours alone with Patrick. Jerry had also promised to show our kids how he cut and ate a pomegranate, and he didn't have time to do that either. We had been on the field two months, and I felt abandoned by Jerry and Janet as well.

Little did we know there had been chatter amongst everyone that weekend because Patrick had recently started a chauffeuring business as another means of supposedly supporting ministry, and he had a 'special guest' coming. The stress was on Patrick to find an armored vehicle for this event, something that was not readily available in the city. After the big event, we discovered the 'special guest' chauffeured by Patrick's business had been none other than Amazon's CEO, Jeff Bezos. No wonder Jerry and Patrick had needed so much time together.

Our Agency back home was of little help. Chad received a few calls from Micah now and then checking in, but Micah and his family were very busy support raising and settling into their new home and his new role in the home office. I reached out to his wife once and didn't hear back for weeks. Janet called me once a month, but she and Jerry were busy support raising, wrapping up their current jobs, selling their house, and moving to another state in their transition to the Agency. Patrick was swamped with church, the chauffer business, his pregnant wife, and shifting. He told everyone on staff to stop asking him for anything. Chad felt he couldn't approach Patrick and ask for team meetings. We didn't know who to turn to.

We were also struggling with handling our finances because the bank Patrick took us to on our pre-trip would not actually make any international wire transfers. We were stuck trying to pay rent, electricity, groceries, and everything else through ATM withdrawals. It was incredibly stressful, and Chad was barking at me to stop paying for groceries with cash. What was I to do if our credit cards weren't working either for the grocery store? We had to eat.

My birthday came and went. Our family went to the zoo and to an "American diner." I wish I could have said it was completely enjoyable, but I felt like I was dying inside. Additionally, I don't know why my birthday was never celebrated in the church's Friday night small group. They always honored special events for everyone else by providing a cake for birthdays, anniversaries, etc. When I saw Heidi next, her comment was, "Oh, it's the birthday person's responsibility to throw the party for everyone else."

I had a phone call from my parents and got to hear my grandpa wish me a happy birthday. I could hardly utter a word in reply as a raging river held inside of me threatened to trickle through the dam wall, resulting in an exploding, cascading force. I had to control it. It wasn't just culture shock. It was neglect, abandonment, and a growing sense of betrayal because of broken team expectations. I felt forgotten and unimportant.

I was so distraught; I stopped brushing my teeth and taking care of regular hygiene. I thought about curling up in the fetal position in the corner of the bedroom, wishing desperately that I could just disappear. I even thought about throwing myself off the fourteenth-floor balcony to escape the pain, chaos, and distress. I was angry with God for leading me here, only to abandon me as well.

I *had* to have connection. I had to have people. I felt no one cared we were even there. No one was there to comfort us.

I remembered the previous month our visiting language teacher had mentioned a homeschool co-op his girls had attended at the local international Christian school, so I looked it up. I started taking my older two kids to this group twice a week, and the youngest joined the preschool on those days. It was three hours in the car, crossing the city in heavy traffic each time we went, but it was the only place Chad and I felt safe leaving our kids. I was desperate for community or a place of belonging, so I started volunteering in the library checking in and shelving books one day a week.

When Patrick and Heidi found out we had plugged into the international Christian school, Patrick sent a text to our entire Agency chat group that we had located the school with all the expats. The comment sounded cheerful and upbeat, but it was actually demeaning and derogatory because there's a negative stigma against missionaries who choose to gather only with other expats while on the field. I was hurt.

We tried to meet with other couples in the church in February. We invited one in particular every single week, but their answer was always no. They were too busy with their ministry tasks. There were no visitors to our home, no other welcome invitations into relationship from other church members, no women's Bible study, no reach out messages to me, nothing.

My Hindu neighbor showed more hospitality welcoming our family into their country and culture than anyone else in the church. She was very sweet and spoke broken English. We went out once together for coffee and to a plant pot stand on the side of a road. She helped me get plants for our home. She let me borrow her beautiful dresses for two different weddings in January, invited us over for tea, cooked various ethnic dishes for us to try, and even had our family over for dinner once.

Besides attending Tuesday morning prayer meetings with the church staff and planning for the music school launch, Chad served on the church's worship team on a regular basis. He was really enjoying playing his trumpet and helping the team. I volunteered to sing harmony on worship team one week and helped with decorations inside the church as well.

In early February, we participated in a community Sports Day at the international Christian school and met some other expat families. It was a welcome sight, and I was eager to meet people I could actually communicate with since half the church we attended couldn't speak English. I wanted to meet some new faces and names and learn tips about surviving this particular field of service. We met a number of them, chatting and gathering any helpful tidbits of information as an expatriate in this city.

Unfortunately, the air was polluted that day, which is possibly why our three-year-old daughter picked up a lung virus the second week of February. Her little chest was heaving rapidly trying to breathe. Patrick came upstairs to see her and immediately recommended a trip to the ER. Seeing his attentive care for our daughter that evening was a refreshing sight.

He took Chad and our daughter to the hospital while I stayed home since our older two were already in bed for the night. I wondered what I had done bringing my children here. Heidi actually messaged me that night and asked how I was doing when my daughter was at the ER. I guess it took an ER visit to finally get their attention. After the hospital visit, Chad and I took our youngest to a local pediatrician and began administering medication via nebulizer at home.

By the end of February, our field team leaders had finally settled into their new flat five floors beneath ours in the same apartment tower. It was comforting to know they were so close rather than a ten-minute Uber drive away. However, my trust had long been broken. Anytime we'd met, it was only about our progress on the music academy. They never really asked how we were doing or if there was anything they could do to help.

When I continued pressing Chad, and he finally felt it was the opportune time to ask the pastor for regular team meetings, we had been on the field for over three months. I was beyond myself feeling overwhelmed by culture shock, isolation, betrayal, and sabotage—although I couldn't have put it to words back then.

A team meeting was scheduled, and we went downstairs to their apartment. We sat on the couch, and I managed to blurt, "There is no support structure here!" Heidi immediately replied, "You have no idea what it was like for me when I first got here!" I then shared my frustration about not being able to connect with the other agency couple when they visited several months ago.

I needed an escape. Chad and I argued about taking a vacation. He was adamant we be there for church on Sunday morning, so we should go during the week. I was adamant to leave over a weekend.

Why did I have to be there every Sunday when Heidi was gone two Sundays in January for their vacation and shifting apartments? Why did I need to follow all the expectations on our list when they hadn't even kept their *one*? What was Heidi doing all day anyway while her kids were in school? She only lived five floors below me but all was silent from her week after week. It wasn't that she didn't make an effort to be a friend, it was the fact that there was no effort being put forth as a field team leader. In all honesty, I needed to take a *week* off with our family!

I didn't trust Patrick and Heidi anymore. I no longer had the desire to serve their church community having been "dropped" on the field and left alone to tread water in survival mode. Chad and I argued a long time, my voice escalating as I begged and pleaded to leave for the weekend. I won the argument. We left for our son's birthday weekend and drove to the south end of town to stay in a hotel.

I was about to break. I pled with the Lord in prayer: *God, if there's something more than this, rescue me!* I fasted for three days, drinking only coffee and water. I broke my fast on a snack we shared with Patrick and Heidi at another "team meeting" to discuss the summer plan for opening the music school. It wasn't a team meeting to ask how we were or what we needed. It was merely a business meeting about the academy...again.

A couple weeks later, Chad and I spent a day rearranging the current music building. Aside from the bakery kitchen, NGO office, and church staff offices, Patrick and Heidi had filled whatever space remained in that building with stuff from their former two-story apartment since they had downsized to a single story flat. Patrick had lost his former office in their home and was also moving it into the building.

We rearranged and tidied the place, preparing for a small Sunday morning crowd. There was an emerging virus and the government was mandating gatherings not to exceed a certain number. The church was setting up both buildings in order to split up the congregation. Patrick and his church staff were very pleased with the transformation we were able to make in such short time!

We carried on as usual those few weeks of March, starting to get into the swing of things. I felt we were making strides with settling into the culture, finding our routine, and finally meeting every Saturday morning with our field team leaders.

There was hope! We could do this. We could hang in there and make it work!

> "We do not want you to be uninformed, brothers and sisters, about the troubles we experienced in the province of Asia. We were under great pressure, far beyond our ability to endure, so that we despaired of life itself. Indeed, we felt we had received the sentence of death. But this happened that we might not rely on ourselves but on God, who raises the dead." 2 Corinthians 1:8-9

CHAPTER 4
EVACUATION

Then it happened. I randomly messaged another American missionary friend how she was doing one Friday morning. She lived on the south side of town, about an hour away. She responded that her stateside agency called in the middle of the night and told her they had booked plane tickets. The US Department of State had just issued a stage four advisory declaring 'Do Not Travel,' and that agency's two teams were to pack their suitcases and evacuate the next day.

We immediately called Jerry to tell him the news. By this time, he and Janet had officially transitioned out of our home church to our Agency. Jerry said we needed to come home. We really wrestled with his decision. We were shocked, and we didn't know what to do.

We conversed with our Agency ED's, one of the global outreach team members from our church (since there was no longer a director), and Patrick and Heidi. I thought to myself, *if they make us leave, I don't think I'll be coming back.* Our family made the decision with the ED's and Patrick and Heidi to stay for the upcoming lockdown.

All parties agreed, and Chad called Jerry to tell him the consensus.

Jerry flew off the handle and demanded we leave the country. He claimed the president of the overall Agency had emailed everyone declaring they evacuate. Later we looked for that email to back up Jerry's claim, and it didn't exist. Each country's regional director made separate decisions, and other nearby missionary families were allowed to make their own decision.

I tried to get Chad to stand up to Jerry and tell him we're staying. After all, we were comfortable in our home, and we didn't have one in the States. We finally had regular team meetings. Plus, the decision had also been made by everyone else. Chad couldn't do it. We acquiesced to Jerry's demands.

We spent the next two to three days trying to get plane tickets because the airport was in process of shutting down completely. Right after Chad filled out the online form and got a flight booked with a credit card that would actually work, we'd receive an email that the flight had been cancelled. This happened flight after flight. Chad even called his mom in the middle of the night to try to use one of her credit cards when ours stopped working from all the strange transactions.

After many attempts and lost hours of sleep, we called our Agency to say we couldn't get tickets. Micah promptly got online. After several attempts with the same result, he was able to secure tickets. Chad and I suffered two nights in a row of only three hours of sleep. We were utterly exhausted.

We didn't know what was happening in the world

around us. We didn't know if by walking through three international airports, we'd pick up this deadly virus and die. No one knew at that early stage. I couldn't wrap my brain around an advisory that said "Do Not Travel" yet we were making plans to travel halfway around the world. It was sheer chaos.

We called the local US embassy because we heard the airport was closed to both outgoing and incoming flights that week, of which we had outbound plane tickets. The embassy agent confirmed the airport was closed. Then why did we have flights? I called the airline, and they confirmed the flight was still operating. We hoped this was true, but there was no way to really know unless we showed up.

All I knew was we didn't have a home to call our own on the other end. I had no idea where we would sleep. I wanted to stay in our current flat and hunker down. It was our home now. After all, Patrick and Heidi lived five stair flights below us in which we could still have access to each other during lockdown. It would finally give us the chance to do the much-needed bonding and relationship repair. I didn't want to exit the country. I was so mad.

We picked up our bags, and I said a quick goodbye to Heidi. We stepped out of our flat and over to the elevator. We left without saying goodbye to our neighbors. We left without saying goodbye to anyone in the church.

We rode the elevator down to the parking garage, climbed into Patrick's van, drove past the apartment community security gate, climbed into the van destined for the airport, and waved goodbye to Patrick as we drove off. In that moment, I thought to myself, *if this is what missions and ministry is all about, I want nothing to do with it.*

The roads, usually crowded and noisy, were eerily empty and lifeless. We arrived at the airport and saw a crowd of foreigners standing around outside the building. I assumed they were all trying to get flights out of the country.

An airline attendant holding a sign with our flight number walked by, and we showed her our booking confirmation. She walked our family into the airport building through a side door. The airport was almost empty. There were just three departing flights left, and the rest of the airport had already shut down. The stores and booths we passed had saran wrap over them. I have never seen that airport emptier than it was that day, and we'd been in and out of that airport seven times before.

We boarded our airplane. I gazed out the window during takeoff wondering, *what in the world is happening? I'm leaving this place. I didn't think I was leaving for two years, yet here I am exiting.*

We had a twelve-hour layover in the first airport and were all able to sleep some. It had been a highly-stressful, grueling few days, and here we were flying halfway around the world. Another passenger was covered head to toe in a hazmat suit, headgear, gloves, and boot coverings. The flights were long, and our youngest very needy. I was exhausted by the sheer amount of sustained adrenaline over the last four months, the lack of sleep over the last several days, the trauma of a sudden evacuation, and the responsibility of tending to a fussy preschooler traveling halfway around the world.

Two more flights with one more layover, and we arrived in our hometown. Chad's parents met us at the airport with their spare pickup truck for us to use, and we drove to a global outreach team member's house to quarantine for fourteen days. This was March 26, 2020.

The next day was our youngest's fourth birthday, and Chad's was to follow a week later. I remember walking on grass for the first time in awe of the thick, lush, soft carpet beneath my feet. I remember turning on the bathroom faucet knowing it was safe to use that water to brush our teeth. And I remember lying in bed staring out the window at the large, beautiful houses in the neighborhood. I wasn't good for much. I was in such a state of shock over the events of the last four months. What just happened?

The other ED Alex's wife reached out to me, but I couldn't respond. Where was she this whole time? I didn't know her, and she didn't know me. She's never messaged me before.

Heidi texted me once during our quarantine to ask how we were. I told her we were trying to figure out where we were going to live next. She never replied. Suddenly, Patrick and Heidi dropped all communication with us. Out of sight, out of mind.

We were isolated there. We went on walks with our kids and drove through DQ a couple times, something we had been missing during our absence. We went for short drives. A couple people dropped food off at the door and managed a quick hello. The night before we left, we were able to have dinner outside with the host couple. I gave good answers to their questions, but quite honestly, I didn't know what else to say. I had been ravaged.

At the end of our quarantine, we moved into Chad's

parent's house. The kids each had a bedroom, and Chad and I slept in their camping trailer. Jerry reached out and said they wanted to come up and debrief with us. I didn't want to see them. I told Chad I had asked Janet could we please meet after three weeks of much-needed time with both sets of our parents. Jerry and Janet came anyway.

I was livid. I felt so controlled by them, angry at the forced evacuation and this forced meeting like we were puppets on a string. I didn't want to see them or anyone else. I had reached the point of avoiding everything and everyone related to the trauma on the field and the evacuation.

Chad told me the meeting would take sixty to ninety minutes. We sat outside in his parent's yard in plastic lawn chairs. The first thing Jerry said in half joking manner was, "How does it feel to be back after only four months with your house just down the street occupied by tenants?" I couldn't believe my ears.

Jerry and Janet then proceeded to tell us they had been appointed as our stateside field team directors in our Agency rather than Joe (the position in charge of Patrick and Heidi's field team). They explained their appointment as field director happened before our evacuation—it just hadn't been announced to us yet. I guess this now justifies our obedience to their evacuation demand?

Then they wanted us to give them our highs and lows. Like I'd really had time to process. At this point, there were no highs. Everything had been too overwhelming. I tried to tell them I felt completely burnt-out, but Janet disagreed with me. She explained 'missionary burnout' happens after a couple years on the field.

When the meeting passed ninety minutes, I impatiently asked how long until we were done? Jerry said the meeting was to be two hours. I was told the meeting was going to be sixty to ninety minutes, and now I needed to get our kids their dinner. I looked over at Chad in disbelief. I had had it. I really couldn't handle one more misfired communication.

Before they left, they gave us a paper explaining why it's not good for us to give negative reporting from the field. I was altogether disenchanted. I felt controlled, voiceless, and like a puppet on their strings. I felt many more things than this I couldn't put into words during that time. The meeting ended tensely.

At this stage in the game, the Jacksons, another member care couple in our Agency, reached out to us and started online video meetings. We had our first meeting with them in his parent's trailer. After our one-week stay at Chad's parent's house, we drove out of state to my parent's house for two weeks. It was wonderful to reconnect with them and receive the love, attention, relationship, and place of belonging we were missing while on the field.

After staying with my parents, we drove back into town and moved into a rental. It was a 1965 house with few upgrades. It had also housed cats who had their way with things, and there were various cobwebs and dead bugs hanging out on the ceilings throughout the home. Our family struggled with allergies and smells during the first couple weeks, but fortunately it was spring and we could keep the windows open most of the day for ventilation from dander and other unpleasant smells. I thought, *we had more sanitary living conditions in our Asian flat!*

The Jacksons of member care drove through town one day and stopped by for a visit. I was still in shellshock. Chad had asked Mr. Jackson in their last online meeting to try to find out from me what were my hesitations about returning to Asia. I hated feeling like I was being labeled as the only one with a problem.

Chad and I also had a phone call with Jerry and Janet in early May while we sat inside the rental house. Chad made it clear to them that he was ready to return when the timing was right, but that I was the reason why we weren't. I self-sabotaged in that moment and spilled that we were arguing a lot on the field and our marriage was part of the problem. Little did I know what this admission would mean to them. Again, I hated feeling like I was being labeled by everyone else as the only one with a problem.

Jerry and Janet scheduled a virtual debrief meeting with the global outreach leadership team at our home sending church. I don't know why Jerry and Janet were leading this meeting as they were no longer staff at our church, but they were there anyway. Jerry's global leadership team still looked to them for leadership and direction.

I remember feeling uncomfortable sharing in front of a panel of ten people that were either new to the global team or who didn't really know us. Staring at those unfamiliar faces on the Zoom screens, I began crying and trying to tell everyone that we didn't have regular field team meetings. Janet quickly stepped in. "Chad and

Claire, why don't you tell the global team what some of your 'big rocks' were on the field?" I went into self-sabotage mode again at her leading and told everyone we were really struggling to communicate between the two of us.

Janet had averted the conversation away from what I was trying to say. She pointed the finger at us and used the information, or admission, of our struggle on the field from our private phone call against us as if the other party had done nothing wrong. Jerry's friend Stan (the executive pastor) concluded the cause of my distress amounted to "culture shock."

I was really hurting over the next week from the results of these conversations. I felt thrown under the bus by Chad and stabbed in the back by Janet during the global outreach team meeting. She congratulated me later via text for really sharing my heart with the team, but I don't see it that way at all.

In fact, I was reminded of a scene from the movie "Ever After" when the servant girl Danielle is dressed as a fairy princess at the ball. The palace court is filled with people decked in attire for the masquerade festivities. Danielle is amongst a crowd of onlookers, facing the prince. In that moment, her stepmother marches up behind her and rips off one of her wings, throwing it on the ground. She demands Danielle tell the prince that she's an imposter—that she's not actually a princess, but rather, she's a common servant girl. This is a vivid picture of how this meeting felt to me. I felt attacked from behind, exposed, and completely disgraced.

As an aside, having returned from the field sustaining

deep wounds, I have grown a respect for those who have served in the military overseas during times of war. I may have a slightly better understanding of what it's like to return from the chaos on the battlefield, only to be disgraced and discarded with little to no 'thank you for your service.' My heart goes out to those wounded warriors who have come home with PTSD and can barely function.

I don't know who these men and women are or if they immediately received the proper care they needed. Maybe these people can't hold a job or support themselves enough to place a roof over their head. These men and women gave *everything* to defend our country physically, and many of them suffer the damages of war the rest of their lives. From the bottom of my heart, thank you for your service.

Comparatively, missionary families give *everything* to fight on the frontlines of a spiritual war, and some certainly face the chaos of clashing cultures and the clamor that exists in harsh, unforgiving environments in overly crowded city jungles around the world. Some of these newly appointed missionaries enter Agencies and field teams with fresh excitement, innocence, and passion to serve the Lord only to face the hard-hearted, tired missionary who may be convicted by their own compromise over the years in light of their new team member.

Additionally, the older missionary might assume the new person doesn't know what they know and certainly hasn't grown a ministry like they've grown, so why listen to them. The new missionary is least expecting to be sabotaged by his or her own leaders, but this does happen. It's happened to me.

Please do not treat wounded warriors returning from the field with avoidance, dishonor, or shame. These men and women deserve utmost respect and continued nurturing back to health until they are healed and functioning once again in society. If you are one of these who have returned from the battlefield—whether physical or spiritual—and have been shamed and treated with dishonor, I want to personally thank you for your service. God sees, and he will reward you.

> "And everyone who has left houses or brothers or sisters or father or mother or wife or children or fields for my sake will receive a hundred times as much and will inherit eternal life." Matthew 19:29

CHAPTER 5

LEAVE OF ABSENCE

S hortly after the disappointing debrief with our church's global outreach leadership team, Chad and I had to decide what to do with his job. He had taken a one-year leave of absence, and while we were still on the field, he had submitted an email requesting a second year. Now that we were suddenly back in the states, his administrator reached out to Chad offering his job back for the upcoming school year. The admin needed to know within the next twenty-four hours. We had to make a very fast, heart-wrenching decision to take the job again since the current status of the world was in lockdown and turmoil for the unforeseeable future.

We informed Jerry, and he promptly drew up a 'leave of absence' form. Again, this Agency side-branch was forming their processes on the fly as we were their "guinea pig" family. Jerry then held a virtual meeting with us and the Agency ED's to explain our decision and his form. The top had reasons why we were taking a leave of absence: to work on our marriage, our communication, and to resolve conflict. He pointed the finger at us too.

The bottom had a long list of expectations, and they were all things *we* had to do. No one else had any responsibilities or expectations to meet during our leave.

And that was it. They left us alone. All of them. They left me in trauma, in heartbreak, in shellshock, in a shipwreck of a field experience, in shame, and they left me voiceless. They didn't provide post-traumatic care, didn't provide any special reading material or recommended missionary retreats for our family. They didn't hold any post-evacuation team meetings to discuss what happened. And we were the ones to blame.

One day in early June, I remember laying down to finally relax on one of the upstairs beds for a short time while Chad took the kids on a bike ride around the neighborhood. There had been few times I was apart from the kids in the last six months. I remember feeling like someone had laid me out on an electrocution table and given me the highest voltage possible. I felt like I was in complete shock I could barely move, barely breathe. I felt like a complete zombie. I took a few concentrated deep breaths and let them out slowly, focusing on relaxing.

Suddenly the doorbell began to ring profusely. I ran downstairs to find our oldest daughter being carried in the door by Chad, and she was hurt badly. Her mouth was bloody and she looked in shock. She had tried to get her bike onto the sidewalk from the road via a driveway, but it was more like a low curb. The bike tire got stuck on the lip and slipped beneath her while she went down hands and face first, breaking both wrists and her two front teeth.

Chad took her to ER and from there straight to the dentist for an emergency root canal. All of a sudden, we had a girl in wrist braces who couldn't even feed herself. Eventually, one wrist brace turned into a cast. Fortunately, it wasn't long before she was able to function on her own. Nevertheless, this occurrence was an added layer of stress and trauma to our already haphazard circumstances.

◈

As we continued to attempt to follow orders on our leave of absence list of expectations, I signed up for counseling sessions from a licensed Christian counselor at a local center. Chad and I continued meetings with the Jacksons, and began biweekly dinner meetings with Stan (the executive pastor) and his wife Jamie for continued check-ins and counseling at Jerry's direction.

I was distressed. I was having heart palpitations, insomnia, difficulty staying calm, difficulty breathing, and outbursts of rage. Loud noises were disruptive and startled me easily. I wasn't showering regularly or brushing my teeth. I'd often leave to go on one-to-two-hour long drives by myself, many times wishing I could drive into the river and end it all. I was suffering.

I was angry and disillusioned by everyone and even by God. While on the field, I felt even God himself had abandoned me. I could feel it happening. My thoughts and emotions in my brain would seep down into my face. Facial muscles would tighten and my jaws would clench. When my face would harden, it would then creep down and grab hold of my heart. Where I once had a soft, loving, and joyful heart, it was hardening and turning cold as stone.

It's like someone turned the lights out. Even though

we had bright, summer sunshine, the world around me went dark. Colors became dull and less vivid.

I lost my trust in people. Suddenly, the world seemed to be filled with evil people who performed wickedly. I could trust no one. I wasn't even sure I could trust God. I have never been so alone in my life, hating myself and hating others.

I would go on walks to sit on a bench and breathe, staring out at the river. Wide and blue, steady and consistent. I tried to take comfort in the sight, but inside was a war zone. Or was I a frozen, empty shell?

My ability to be a wife and mother suffered greatly. I couldn't cook, couldn't clean the house. Chad bore the load of chores and parenting over half of the time as I struggled to get out of bed.

I stopped reading my Bible. I had no desire to read any books at all. I couldn't pray. The only prayer I could pray was, "Help me," in a whisper just barely escaping my lips as I lay on my bed. I've never experienced that level of physical, emotional, spiritual, mental, or relational exhaustion before.

❖

Another month went by, and I reached out to Janet again. I was ready to talk and needed help processing. Jerry and Janet drove up again for another meeting with us. They sat in our backyard, and Jerry told us, "Jesus Christ loves you." I brought up the missing team meetings issue again, and he simply stated, "Patrick said you had team meetings." End of discussion. Janet hinted at the notion that I needed to "die to self."

In regard to our difficulty with Heidi I was told, "Heidi wasn't going to be your friend. I know you had that hope. You'll have to change your expectations." Then they drove home. I tried to let that meeting encourage me, but it really didn't. I knew something was wrong, and I felt it. This was the second meeting to go awry...or was it the fourth?

I emailed the two ED's at the Agency home office expressing my desire to debrief with them, and that I felt we had lost that relationship with them when Jerry and Janet became our direct "bosses." They tried to understand and held a meeting with one in attendance, but I don't think they understood. At the time, I knew something felt wrong, but I didn't fully understand in a way I could explain either.

I felt Jerry was still our church's global outreach director because that's how he started. Somehow things rapidly changed while we were away. We couldn't wrap our minds around not having someone at our church. Now he was our main point of contact in our Agency, taking over the former communications we had with the two new ED's.

Our sending church didn't fill his vacated position, and we didn't know who to talk to. To be honest, the global outreach team including Stan still looked to Jerry for direction regarding our situation. Where we once had three separate 'legs' of support: Patrick and Heidi (field team), Alex and Micah (Agency ED's), and Jerry and Janet (home sending church global outreach director)— this shifting of roles left us standing on only one support leg—Jerry and Janet—and everyone else was now looking to them for direction.

We also reconnected with a couple in our hometown who were part of a different field team in this small Agency branch. The Spencers were incredibly friendly and even had our family over for dinner one evening. They were trying to recruit us into their field team within this Agency in a different part of Asia.

I met with the wife Kathy on more regular occasions to share my distress, grief, and pain over what had happened and keeping her up to date on the communications. Over time, she and her husband became well aware of what was going on.

In September, Patrick and Heidi reached out to Chad and me, asking for help designing their church's stage area since they had flipped the room around to the other end. They had also located another space for rent a few doors down from their church so they had a new office building for the staff.

I drew a few pictures of what the stage could look like with recommended colors and materials and a potential furniture placement plan for their office's main space and sent them to Heidi. Chad discussed sound system and technology with Patrick. Chad and I were happy they found a new building and wished we were still there to help with set up, although we were happy to contribute to this project from a distance. After all, that's what we were working on with them while on the field.

◆

Another school year started, and I homeschooled the older two kids while the youngest attended a nearby preschool. Since we were in the States for the next school year, we had purchased the rental before they sold it out from under us and we had to move yet again. We started remodeling. When it was completed after three months, we moved our dishes into the kitchen the first week of October. We were finally settled after our evacuation from Asia. We had been moving around, living in four different houses for six months.

We randomly had a short phone call one day that fall with Patrick and Heidi. Patrick started with a very brief, "I'm sorry we left for a week in January." That was it. They wanted to know if we were returning. Chad was excited, but I shared that God would have to "reconfirm for me" our return to this field team. Why would I return to this team if the only communication we received from them in the six months following evacuation was if we could help them with their stage and one phone conversation with a half-apology to see if we were coming back?

The truth is, Chad and I would often discuss and dream of a return to the mission field. The only holdup for me was the Agency. I needed to feel like I was part of a team and what I had to say mattered. I needed to know I wasn't just someone else's pawn.

By mid-October, I was willing to try one more meeting with Jerry and Janet. After all, our apartment on the field was still intact, and we were still paying for it from our Agency account. It had been useful for the ministry there, so that was a bonus. Patrick and Heidi's family had lived in it for several months, including the time they had their new baby. Another family lived in our flat for a month as they were completing their adoption process. In addition, a single man was soon arriving on the field to join the Agency team, with plans of living in our flat for a month or two until he secured his own.

For this final meeting, determinedly, I was prepared with a specific list to discuss with Jerry and Janet as recommended by my counselor. We began driving to their new hometown, and four hours later, we first met at a local coffee shop with the Jacksons of member care who also happened to be in town.

We sat down with our coffee drinks in a small room. The Jacksons asked what we hoped to get out of the upcoming meeting with Jerry and Janet. I said we hoped to feel validated. They agreed that was a wonderful goal then counseled us to be prepared if we didn't get the result we were wanting.

Then we all went to Jerry and Janet's new home for lunch. After a short tour of their new home and a delicious lunch, the Jacksons took off for their hometown. I desperately wanted to ask them to stay and listen. I wanted them to mediate and help guide the conversation if I didn't feel heard yet again.

The meeting started off with a bang. I had my list of six things to address and was immediately put on the spot to share first. Following a wonderful, hospitable lunch, I wasn't particularly up to the task of confrontation. Doing it myself alone was also daunting. Chad didn't really understand me. Uneasily, I started with, "We'd like to feel validated." I quickly listed all six items from my list. I got one nod of response from Janet after stating we were hurt by the way they handled the debrief meeting with our sending church's global outreach leadership team.

After I finished, she responded, "So, tell me why you felt it was so difficult to communicate between the two of you?" I answered her question. I didn't realize until later that the items on the list regarding the conflict we had with them had been completely avoided. Chad knew in the moment, but didn't help steer the conversation back to discussion on my points either.

Then it was their turn to talk. Jerry advised us not to become bitter because the enemy would want us to stay in that place. He stated, "The field is what it is, and you'll have to decide if you want to be part of it." He offered us a position of general service back on that field, but not specifically a music school project.

I then shared my thoughts about needing a weekly meeting with a member care woman while on the field, and Janet immediately responded, "Oh, it would never be enough." I shared my thoughts on being on the field nine or ten months of the year and two to three months stateside, and her response was, "You know missionaries used to ship themselves over in coffins because they never expected to return." I felt my ideas instantly overridden as she shared her expertise. I literally had nothing to contribute to the forming and shaping of this team.

Janet then proceeded to tell a story about how she was really mad at another national partner for not following through on their expected task on the calendar. She explained how she had chosen to forgive that person without confrontation. She didn't explain why she told us that story or how that directly applied to our situation, and we weren't smart enough to ask any clarifying questions as to what she meant. It was very passive-aggressive. Chad and I both interpreted the meaning of her illustration to be this: we must forgive the national partners without confronting them.

We left that meeting, and Chad felt good. I couldn't sleep that night. Insomnia struck yet again. I tried to explain to Chad when he woke up how they completely avoided the confrontation. He too had noticed during the meeting but thought it got resolved when I appeared satisfied. We realized later it takes me longer to process. I thought maybe we could attempt conflict resolution with them one more time the next day before we were to drive home.

We asked to meet once more. Again, Chad didn't really understand my need. In between this request to meet and our original intention to try to resolve conflict yet again, I began to question myself. Was I in the wrong? Was I being prideful? Demanding? Bitter? Was I being rebellious against the spiritual authorities in my life? Since I felt all alone in what I was trying to accomplish, I ultimately decided to take Janet's advice from her story and do the "super spiritual" thing to try to forgive the national partners without needing to resolve conflict. When we met one more time, we enjoyed tea and cookies, had a friendly talk, and avoided any tender issues.

We drove home that afternoon, and I was completely done. I just couldn't swallow or absorb what had happened on the field or during our leave because it was absolutely enormous. The wounds and battle scars were bleeding, gaping holes. Chad was actually thinking our meetings went well and we were on the road to return with the team! Each encounter with these people was leaving me with additional angst.

I felt like they were conditioning us to comply. I felt like I was being asked to erase my identity and autonomy in order to stay on this team. They had shared their stance and presented the ultimatum. Stay silent and raise no issue. Just do as you're told to serve this ministry.

We had tried multiple times with them, but it wasn't going to be any other way but theirs. I wished I could explain and convince them otherwise, but they had their beliefs about how things should be, and I had mine. They weren't willing to listen or work with us, therefore, we became incompatible.

I felt disoriented. I questioned my sanity. Finally, I concluded that compliance would require me to betray my very sense of being, and I couldn't do it. They needed someone more agreeable than me, apparently.

I didn't think trust could break down any further, but I was yet to be surprised.

> "If your brother or sister sins, go and point out their fault, just between the two of you. If they listen to you, you have won them over." Matthew 18:15

CHAPTER 6
GRIEVANCE LETTER

"But if they will not listen, take one or two others along, so that 'every matter may be established by the testimony of two or three witnesses.'" Matthew 18:16

Over the next month, I battled insomnia in a serious way. I'd wake up at two or three am and be up for hours. My brain wouldn't shut off—the alarm bells were resounding so loudly. Something was majorly wrong and needed to be fixed. The invalidation from Jerry and Janet was overwhelming. The emotional neglect was abusive.

The whole experience was beyond my ability to cope. I started typing a letter listing all the difficulties we faced because I needed Jerry and Janet to validate what happened or at least attempt to discuss or work through what happened. And maybe, just maybe, I was hoping to hear the words, "I'm sorry," come out of their mouths.

We communicated with Jerry, Janet, and the two Agency ED's in early December that we needed to meet to iron out some things in order to discuss our return to the field at the end of the school year. Jerry questioned why we needed to bring the two ED's into the conversation, probably thinking whatever needed to be discussed, he and Janet could handle. No meeting was scheduled.

I continued writing the letter. It was a super clear method of communicating the unaddressed, unresolved problems. I wanted to fully express our experience with all the bumps and challenges so that the Agency would recognize and address areas of weakness in order to build trust within this team. This discussion would reassure me this wouldn't happen again. It would show me what I had to say or how I felt mattered to the team. How else could I feel any validation, comfort, or resolution? How else could they proactively fix the issues so this wouldn't happen to the next unsuspecting party?

Chad saw my distress and was willing to help me. After hours of writing and editing, mostly in the middle of the night, the end result was a well-written, transparent yet humble four-page grievance letter from both of us. It was pretty straight forward. The debate now was: *do we send it?*

We talked for hours about a return to our field. We wanted to return, but it required working with this team in order to do so. Ultimately, I couldn't meet the expectation to forgive without addressing the problems or at least hearing an apology from Jerry and Janet, Patrick and Heidi. It was too big. It was a looming mountain on top of me, crushing me by its weight, waking me in the night, and occupying my mind the entire day.

We shared the letter with the Jacksons and Stan and Jamie at our home church. The Jacksons said it was written well and that all parties could learn from it. Stan seemed surprised by the letter, but agreed it was good communication. The Spencers (who live minutes away from our home) also knew what was happening in the Agency. Although we hadn't specifically shared our letter with them, I was meeting regularly with Kathy for support and encouragement. They'd been following along our journey.

We communicated again with everyone in January 2021 that we needed to work through some issues before discussing a return to the field. Thinking we were following the leave of absence expectation that Jerry had given us to 'resolve conflict,' Chad took a short phone call with Jerry. It was an upbeat, friendly conversation in which Jerry again offered a spot for our family on the field team. Since Jerry had dinner guests arriving soon, Chad decided not to broach conflict during this phone call, especially since everyone was not present and hearing. Chad told Jerry he'd be sending along the information that would need further discussion.

We emailed our grievance letter to the two Agency ED's, Jerry and Janet the evening of January 21, 2021. At this point, we knew we needed to involve the next level of leadership if problems were to be acknowledged and dealt with appropriately.

The next day, the Agency ED's emailed a reply to schedule a meeting with us. Chad messaged Jerry asking if he got our letter. Jerry texted, "I don't know what to say."

Two days after sending the letter, we hopped on a virtual meeting with the Agency ED's. They asked if I had written the letter, or if Chad had also written the letter.

We stated we both wrote the letter. They gave us a short apology. Then they questioned my calling. Finally, Micah stated he would ask the Jacksons to mediate between Jerry and Janet and us.

Then it went quiet. We waited for a meeting to be scheduled. By this point, I felt the urgency to receive communication from the Agency. Each day that went by felt painstaking. I was about to explode. I asked Chad if he'd heard from the Jacksons. He said no. As the days crawled by and no communication was made with our family, I began sensing a mediatory meeting was being avoided in typical fashion.

My birthday came, and I was met that morning with messages from Patrick and Heidi asking if they could move a large number of our furniture items from our flat to their new house in the south end of the city. They were shifting yet again and were taking our car with them too. Chad greeted me that morning with questions about Patrick and Heidi taking our stuff from our apartment, not a 'happy birthday.' I was upset. I felt used.

The ED's finally told us Jerry and Janet had come down with COVID and couldn't meet. There was no communication that a meeting would be planned at all. The mediatory meeting had been avoided.

I sent two blunt emails to the Agency ED's, Jerry, and Janet. I communicated multiple frustrations. I was beyond myself. I wanted to discuss what a "team meeting" actually meant! There was no response. My two short emails were probably just the ammunition Jerry and Janet needed to present me to the ED's as the bitter, rude party who was no longer emotionally stable or fit for service.

Instead of scheduling a mediatory meeting with the Jacksons, we received an email from the ED's the next day—only thirteen days after submitting our grievance letter—stating the Agency and our home sending church had talked (Alex and Stan), and they had decided to dismiss our family. Reasons given were due to COVID, the music academy project was no longer available, and they couldn't find another field of service that matched our skills and abilities. They told us we were supposed to "glorify God." They told us to submit our resignation to the HR department.

Chad and I made several conclusions. First, these people didn't really know us. Second, they didn't care to find out what other skills we had. And third, they didn't work with us to look elsewhere for a placement. They didn't even know that two other fields within this smaller Agency branch had already been trying to recruit us!

Not only were they dismissing us from their Agency branch, but they were sending us straight to HR to submit our resignation from the larger organization altogether. Did Alex even have that authority? If Jerry and Janet couldn't have us, then they made sure no one else could either?

Another arrow drawing its death blow went through my heart. I sent Alex, the lead ED, a couple direct messages that morning stating my distress and alarm at their decision and sudden change of course. I wrote of Jerry and Janet, "They never apologized!"

We met with the Stan and Jamie for dinner again. Stan told us on behalf of Jerry and Janet, "It would take four hours to go through your letter, and they don't have time for that." The excuse was Jerry and Janet were busy traveling and had their own ministry so they didn't have time for us. I thought to myself, *WE are part of your ministry!* Stan reiterated the importance of reconciling with Jerry and Janet and quoted the scripture: "as far as it depends on you, live at peace with everyone" (Romans 12:18). He said, "Hurt people hurt people." Was this another excuse not to discuss?

A week later, the ED Micah sent us an email stating we do what was necessary to wrap up the apartment and our belongings that were left on the field eleven months prior. Another arrow. We felt so controlled, like we had absolutely no say in what was happening. It felt like a dictatorship.

We initiated one final phone conversation with Patrick and Heidi to attempt conflict resolution and offer to come serve. We proposed being "sent" directly from our home church rather than through the Agency. We mentioned how we were hurt on the field but that went nowhere. They weren't willing to listen. Patrick couldn't understand why I had trauma. He said, "I travel back and forth from my country to the US all the time. Can you please explain why you think you have trauma?" It was completely invalidating. I'm not sure a national pastor understands what it's like to leave the US and enter into the country or culture they grew up in anyway. Patrick told us, "You came to be served and not to serve." He told us Chad was "called," but I wasn't. He said we were trying to exit the country at the time of our evacuation when I reached out to my other missionary friend and called Jerry. What?

I shared with Kathy Spencer what had happened, and

she wondered if she and her husband should say something on our behalf to the Agency core team (ED's and field team leaders). In the end, they stayed quiet. Apparently, there's risk to one's own position or status within the Agency should one speak up. The alternative is to remain silent and stay on the good side of those in power.

We requested a follow up meeting with the ED's. They were traveling at the time to an "Iron Sharpens Iron" conference (I find this ironic). They both hopped on a video call with us. With tears, I apologized if any of my email communications hurt Jerry and Janet's feelings. Alex had a huge smile on his face. It was silent for a few seconds as he sat there on the couch soaking up my tear-streamed apology. The next thing Alex said was, "Yeah, I talked to Jerry, and he said he had apologized to you." The aura of the moment snapped. I was in disbelief at what I was hearing. I prodded Chad on the side of his leg. Jerry had lied to Alex which had influenced Alex's decision to fire us. We said nothing, and the meeting ended.

We tried all we could to get a meeting scheduled to "reconcile" with Jerry and Janet as the Agency called it. We pursued the request for a meeting, asking one of the ED's to please mediate this meeting between us and Jerry and Janet. They had not spoken with us since receiving our grievance letter. Alex, the lead ED, agreed and scheduled the "reconciliation" meeting.

The day of the meeting, I reached out to the Agency secretary to ask for my email password. She said she was no longer part of the Agency. She shared her story of being intimidated by Alex in the home office and forced out. Then he lied about her in the group chat saying she had "resigned" when he'd essentially fired her. Hearing this from the former secretary just about did me in.

When Chad returned home that afternoon, he told me Alex called him while he was at work. Alex told Chad it would be good if we came to this "reconciliation" meeting with a humble apology for Jerry and Janet like we had done in our last meeting with him. He stated there wouldn't be time to work through the issues in our letter. Basically, Alex told us we weren't going to be given the chance to discuss our letter with Jerry and Janet. I was being told what to say and how to communicate. I wasn't going to do it.

It was a combination of communication from the former secretary and Alex's guidelines for the meeting that caused me to tailspin that afternoon. I told Chad about what happened to their former secretary. Chad and I argued about the meeting. I refused to attend based on Alex's guided expectations.

Chad went to the meeting alone. He was super frustrated with me. I listened from the top of the stairs for a moment as I started recording the conversation. They asked where I was, and why I wasn't in the meeting. Chad stated, "I don't know." Jerry and Janet reiterated, "You told us it was your marriage that was the problem." They stated, "You didn't practice Matthew 18."

I couldn't listen anymore. I went into my room and shut the door to read books to my youngest daughter. When the meeting was almost done, I went back into the upstairs hallway to stop the phone recording. I heard laughing and joking from Jerry. "We *love* the Larsens, but we don't like your kind of coffee, Chad!" (This was in reference to the cheap brand Chad would drink). Then they wrapped up the meeting and said goodbye.

I felt completely set up. Swindled, really. *Used and abused*. Spiritually trafficked, yes. The whole thing was never about stewarding our family's mission to bring the gospel to the nations. It had only been about what our family could contribute through the BAM to the national pastor's ministry and our puppet-like status with Jerry and Janet.

I remember one morning I was kneeling on the ground in heartache and in tears, shifting items on the floor in our pantry. Out of the blue I heard in my spirit the words, *"It's not your fault."* That was it. I knew the Lord was speaking to my heart, comforting me and letting me know I wasn't a failure.

CHAPTER 7

AGENCY OLIGARCHS

C had continued to try conversing with Alex regarding our situation since he had promised there would always be an "open door of communication." Chad got on the phone with Alex to attempt to explain why I chose not to attend the "reconciliation" meeting and what we had learned from his secretary. He made sure to tell us his secretary was lying.

I sent an email to Alex, Micah, Jerry and Janet at some point in April apologizing to Jerry and Janet, trying to explain myself, and asking clarifying questions. No one replied.

I messaged Alex with a question. If "the door of communication is always open," then why had Janet not read any of my text messages since February? My messages were literally never opened. He curtly responded, "There have been many open doors and opportunities for communication, but you have chosen to not take advantage of those. What you are demanding now is communication on your terms."

I couldn't believe what I was reading. None of what

he said was true! Did he really believe what he was saying? I was baffled.

We were the ones to communicate openly in meetings and in our grievance letter. We requested mediation with Jerry and Janet. We were the ones to follow up multiple times to schedule a "reconciliation" meeting after we'd been fired. He was the one that called to tell us to apologize and that we would not work through our letter in that meeting. Was I really "demanding communication on my terms," or were they demanding it on theirs? I'm pretty sure the opposite presentation of factual information and twisting the true state of reality, making something appear a certain way when it's actually not, is called gaslighting.

We ended up scheduling one last video meeting with Alex. I had a small list of confrontational questions to ask him. Chad spent an hour laying out his plea to Alex and sharing his heart while I sat and listened. At the end, Alex said, "Even Paul wanted to go to certain places but was prevented." I sat there incredulous that Chad was trying to get Alex to let us back in. I had to leave early anyway to take our son to the dentist for an appointment, so I said goodbye. My questions were left unasked.

I was completely done with this group. I was sick of their tactics. I couldn't believe they were representing missions and "stewarding" God's call to the Great Commission he had placed on people's lives.

Continued arguments over our belongings ensued. Patrick wanted us to donate our vehicle to his ministry, and all the rest of our household was to be absorbed by their ministry as well. I felt completely used. It became very obvious to me they were more concerned about gaining our things than inviting us back to the field... of which we had been trying to do. Unfortunately, any chance of a quick, healthy recovery, streamlined conflict resolution, or restorative return to the field had been rapidly backpedaling due to the ineptitude of our "leaders."

Finally, we communicated with Stan and Jamie during another dinner meeting that we weren't sure we were done with that field. We were super frustrated others were closing the door on us when we weren't sure this was actually the Lord's will. We might have a return in our future with another agency and needed to retain our belongings rather than transfer them to Patrick and Heidi. Stan agreed.

Chad and I then began talking about the possibility of moving over from the small branch within the Agency to the larger organizational body in case there was another team we didn't know about in that country. Chad got in touch with our pre-field counselor to discuss switching back over to the main body and what needed to be done. This man suggested calling and talking with the Vice President of the company.

Chad had a couple friendly phone conversations with the VP asking questions and gathering information on how to move from the smaller Agency branch to the larger body of the organization. Unfortunately, there was no other team from the larger organization in that country. I begged Chad to tell him what had happened within the side-branch of the Agency, but he never did.

Shockingly, it was at this time that we discovered on our Agency social chat that many of the core leadership team flew or drove into our city from across the country for a luncheon at our home church. Chad saw the posted video and noticed we had been promptly removed from the chat after that. No one told us they had gathered together, even though we had met with Stan and Jamie *that very evening* for dinner. Stan didn't tell us at dinner that they had all met together for lunch at our church. The Spencers didn't tell us and neither did Chad's member care mentor Mr. Jackson. They were all there—Jerry, Janet, Stan, the ED's, Mr. Jackson, and Mr. Spencer—only five miles away from our house.

Our hearts were heavily grieved yet again. This left me with no choice. The VP of the larger Agency *had* to know! At the end of April, I drafted and sent an email to the VP and a few of the other home office executive staff, telling them the short version of what happened within the small branch of their organization.

It was actually our ED Alex that sent a defensive email reply to the group. He didn't believe what I had said or how I described it. Chad and I drafted a response to Alex, stating we wished their Agency branch would have met with us when their core leadership team all gathered in our home church. We communicated we wished they would have practiced their own four core values in their dealings with our family.

This was when the VP got involved. He worked with Alex to find every communication we had made or reason why they could put the blame on our family for our 'forced' resignation. They pointed to an email Chad

had written apologizing for his own weakness that Chad had actually been guided to write at the direction of his member care counselor Mr. Jackson. I was livid. I couldn't believe the member care mentor would coerce Chad to write an apology for his own weaknesses, and then the Agency use it against us.

The VP also twisted my words from my email saying that we agreed to resign when I had simply stated we had "no other choice but to resign." With this comment in mind, Alex made sure to mention the grievance policy in the handbook in his next email. Thinking the 'formal grievance policy' was an option to sorting out this mess, I spent hours upon hours creating an 'official grievance letter', much of it written during the night hours…again.

However, Chad and I ultimately concluded the larger Agency's official grievance process would be pointless with the VP as the head of this panel. He had already chosen sides with Alex and demonstrated that by his email communications. We didn't want to be part of this team or organization anyway if this was the way the leadership—from top to bottom—treated their people! We also didn't want a grievance letter put on our file which might threaten our chances of joining a different agency in the future.

We wrote one last email stating our case, refuting all of Alex's and the VP's arguments. We stated we believed they conspired together in order to kick us out in retaliation over our grievance letter. We definitely received a warning text message from Stan at our home church who had read and disapproved of our last email. Stan told us that we had tried to "go around the authority" of the side-branch by calling the VP to transfer back to the larger organization.

Ultimately, the VP threw up his hands and gave the excuse that he didn't know all the conversations that had gone on. It was done. There was nothing else we could do but gulp down a forceful, humiliating resignation from this Agency.

When our account finally rolled over into "resigned" status on May 31, 2021, I spent all of June trying to iron out our Agency financial account before it was officially called a wrap. We had been paying out of pocket for our apartment rent, wiring funds overseas directly to the landlord. In turn, Patrick would reimburse us with Agency funds through his US bank. It was so messed up. Strangely, we hadn't received reimbursement for the prior four months nor for the amount the adoptive family had contributed to help with rent during their month-long stay in our flat. Patrick had also been drawing money out monthly from our Agency account to cover other expenses he had on the field such as apartment cleaning, car cleaning, and whatever else came up.

Working with the head of finance in our Agency, we calculated numbers and discovered Patrick owed us about $10,000 either directly or transfer from Patrick's account to ours. In my opinion, he was probably hoping none of this got sorted out. He would have gotten away with his mismanagement of funds by withholding rent reimbursement from us and leeching withdrawals out of our Agency ministry account with no receipt reporting or accountability.

The finance director was caught in the middle of this

mess. These were not his best days in office, I'm sure of that. When all was said and done, what small amount was left in our account we requested to be dispersed to four other missionary accounts whom we knew or met at trainings during pre-field. The finance department honored our request.

We contacted the international Christian school on our field, and one of their staff organized movers to pack and shift everything from our apartment into a storage warehouse. The school had already done this for a dozen other expat families that also evacuated the year prior due to COVID. This man also picked up the vehicle from Patrick and gave it to a pregnant teacher for their family to use.

My anger festered into rage at the injustice of our situation. How dare they invite our family to the mission field and then leave us to tread water alone! How dare they ignore our trauma and shellshock! How dare they silence us, conceal the real issues, steal our mission, and steal our Agency commissioning! How dare they attempt to absorb all our household belongings, vehicle, and even our Agency finance account for their ministry! How dare they place all blame on the 'scapegoat' and send us packing into the desert wasteland! I felt completely devoured. I wanted justice. I wanted a pain and suffering settlement.

I visited a local attorney, a childhood friend of Chad's, near the end of the school year. We sat down in the consult room, and he asked a bunch of questions. I didn't have anything concrete to provide. His conclusion at the end of our meeting was, "Don't waste your summer on this. Go enjoy your family. You don't want the mental or emotional weight of a court case."

Holding back tears and keeping a stoic, professional face, I nodded in agreement. I knew at this very moment there was nothing left that I could do on my own to seek justice or fairness regarding the hand we'd been dealt by the members of our Agency. Every abuse, every insult, and every invalidating comment had sent an arrow in my back or through my heart. I was covered in them.

CHAPTER 8

PASTORS AND ELDERS

"If they still refuse to listen, tell it to the
church; and if they refuse to listen even
to the church, treat them as you would a
pagan or a tax collector." Matthew 18:17

In September, Chad asked our current head pastor
Jacob and our music director Drake (also one of our
small group leaders of three years) if he could come
in and meet with them. I chose not to attend, or I might
have entered the church building and started yelling,
screaming, crying, or punching someone. Chad said the
head pastor expressed his understanding why we needed
to attend a different fellowship in order to heal.

Our friend Drake agreed and even admitted that Stan
had called Jerry after every dinner meeting we'd have
with him and his wife over a period of nine months.
Given Stan was good friends with Jerry while on church
staff together, Stan would tell Jerry what we shared at our
dinner meetings, and Jerry would immediately 'refute'
what we said. It appeared their days in the office were

met with juicy morsels of gossip while excluding us from those conversations.

When Chad told me what our music director admitted was happening inside the church offices, I decided I'd had enough with Stan as well. He was another one of Jerry's puppets! I wrote an email to the head pastor Jacob and music director Drake. They didn't reply, so ten days later I sent a follow up. This time, Drake offered a few comforting words via email but that was it.

I decided to go full circle and communicate with the very last level of leadership in our home church since Stan had lost my trust, the head pastor never responded to me, and the music pastor simply shrugged his shoulders while briefly giving me well wishes. This matter needed to go before the elders of the church.

Chad wrote an email to the elders, and the head elder responded by saying what we communicated was not what Stan and Drake had reported had happened. I was incredulous. Why would Drake stand before the elders to give a report on us when he hadn't even reached out to us or heard our story?

I responded to the elders and suggested that "the testimony of two or three witnesses" (Matthew 18:16) had not actually occurred because Drake was not a witness, we were! They asked if I wanted to meet, and I said yes. In preparation for the meeting, I compiled a timeline of events and all email communications into a folder.

Two of the elders met Chad and me at a park shelter next to a river one cold day in October. The four of us sat at the picnic table together. They listened for a long time, validated our pain, and shared their love. It was a comforting meeting.

However, their simple synopsis was issues were being "swept under the rug." They said that Jerry and Janet had "moved on" from the church so there was no need to try to pursue anything (even though they are still supported by the church, preach at the church, and host some of the church's missions activities including ongoing trips to Patrick and Heidi). The elders encouraged us that God would avenge.

I handed them the folder and a copy of the book *The Subtle Power of Spiritual Abuse* by David Johnson and Jeff VanVonderen. I don't know if anyone at our home church ever read it. That was our final parting meeting with our home sending church of fourteen years. It was yet another layer of grief that I didn't expect.

Walking home from the park meeting that day, I realized I had done absolutely everything I could to get my voice heard or search for any morsel of relief from the injustice. I desperately wanted someone to hold these leaders accountable in all three of our 'support legs': field team, Agency, and home church.

I never expected to find myself hanging on for dear life to the bottom rung of the hierarchy ladder, only to discover my lack of subjection and compliance to authorities got my fingers stomped on until I fell off completely. There was nothing left to do. No one stepped in as mediator or representative on our behalf. And these are pastors.

Their inaction left me helpless, defenseless, and with no other choice but to turn this mountain of suffering over to the Lord. This was going to take some time. I didn't know how things would ever change. I didn't know if I would be able to heal from this. I didn't know how to recover. I didn't know whether I'd be trapped inside this nightmare for the rest of my life.

I retreated into myself. Who else could understand what had happened? Which of my close friends have gone through this? Who could relate? I put up walls and hid inside them. I wanted to shut out the world. I wanted to fly away, anywhere, to escape the overwhelming pain. There was no one to comfort, no one to understand me. They had all walked away and left me broken-hearted and bleeding on the wayside.

I was challenged to succumb to the pressures of an all-consuming darkness of hatred, rage, and revenge. I was challenged to reject the faith on account of the failures and sins of men abusing their positions of power, cutting off our ministry, and exploiting our weaknesses all while claiming to represent Christ.

All I could do was cry and drag myself through the motions of life day after day. Days turned into weeks, weeks turned into months, and months turned into years. I was a broken person. Although no one would suspect it when I was with them, they didn't know that whenever I was alone, I couldn't stop the tears.

CHAPTER 9

ROAD TO HEALING

"The Lord is close to the brokenhearted
and saves those who are crushed in spirit."
Psalm 34:18

During the month of May we engaged with a special organization called MRI (Missionary Resource International) for pastoral care and counseling at the direction of my licensed Christian counselor. We were assigned a team of two, a man and a woman, that met with Chad and me on video calls. We really felt they heard us, validated us, prayed for us, and counseled us as best they could during the time we were communicating with the Agency VP.

We realized pastoral care was what we needed all along! They were there for us when we had no other support. We forwarded one of the VP's email responses to us, and they were also grieved and apologized for the way the Agency was handling us. They seemed to know as if this was a common occurrence.

In July we attended Sonscape Retreats for pastors

and missionaries in another state. It was here we received wonderful pastoral care and prayer. It was here we learned there were "unhealthy ministries and healthier ministries." I noticed they gave no claim to a completely "healthy" ministry.

I remember sitting in one of the sessions struggling to hold back a torrent of emotion. I thought I would burst and start wailing in front of everyone. We were recommended a book on grief. The pastor also recommended we find another church body in which to heal since our current church had retained strong ties to Patrick, Heidi, Jerry, Janet, and the Agency.

One evening at Sonscape, we shared a bit of our story with another pastor and his wife during free time, and this pastor said it sounded like gaslighting. This was the validation Chad needed to hear after months of trying to tell him we were in a toxic relationship!

About this time, one of the national couples from Patrick and Heidi's church on the field reached out to us. They had just left the Asian church staff and were grieving as well. We reconnected and began conversing weekly which was a comfort for both of us. We compared notes about our wounds and realized the incredibly deep state of this spiritually fallen ministry, still hidden today behind the façade of gospel-oriented speech.

She also shared they had to get permission from Patrick and Heidi if they were able to spend any time with our family while we were on the field. Our whole situation was being carefully monitored and controlled by our leaders, and, unfortunately, we had been left alone on the field much of the time. These conversations were continued confirmation and a comfort to me.

More importantly, this relationship provided the companionship necessary for processing, healing, accountability, and recovery. We both wanted so badly to heal from the wounds inflicted by an unhealthy ministry but didn't really know how or where to start. Fortunately, Chad and I were able to pass along a few nuggets we had learned through MRI and Sonscape Retreats with this sweet couple.

My Asian friend and I pulled out *The Grief Recovery Handbook* by John W. James and Russell Friedman and began the book study together. God did not leave us alone in our sorrow, but rather, reconnected us for this very purpose. Recovery and healing seemed daunting. Reading and talking were a Godsend for both of us. We were able to encourage one another and shepherd each other through the process of grief recovery while following through on the assignments.

The first assignment was to make an overview of our lives and plot significant events on a timeline. After sharing and talking through our event timelines, we began approaching the chapter on forgiveness and closure letters. Uh-oh.

Forgiveness is a word that makes people cringe or pretend they didn't hear. In addition, praying for your enemies is a ridiculous task no one has time for either, right? I know I've had to wrestle through my own need to forgive, especially when it seemed others had placed upon my shoulders a looming mountain of pain and an ocean of grief I didn't ask for and never wanted!

I admit it took me a while to obey. The holidays were a busy distraction. Other things won over my time and attention, so it was easy to avoid altogether.

It wasn't until I suffered a horrible ankle sprain in early January and was laid up in bed that I knew it was time. Don't wait as long as I did or you might suffer an ankle sprain as well in order to get you to sit still and do it! I was a captive audience.

Regarding forgiveness, I've often wondered if God calls those in his 'kingdom of priests' (Revelation 1:6, 5:10) to intercede for the sins of others just as Christ did for us. When people heap abuse on others, slap on a label titled "scapegoat," and send them outside of the camp to die, how are we to view the situation?

I believe to "bear iniquity" is to absorb unmerited blame and punishment, taking it upon oneself, and releasing the need to hold the other party responsible for the debt they owe. In light of Christ's similar predicament, I might come to the conclusion that to bear his image brings honor and glory to God.

> "Yet it was the Lord's will to crush him and cause him to suffer, and though the Lord makes his life an offering for sin, he will see his offspring and prolong his days, and the will of the Lord will prosper in his hand. After he has suffered, he will see the light of life and be satisfied; by his knowledge my righteous servant will justify many, and he will bear their iniquities." Isaiah 53:10-11

Taking it a step further, Jesus says, "But I tell you, love your enemies and pray for those who persecute you" (Matthew 5:44). God reveals to his people through the life and words of Jesus that forgiveness and intercession for those who sin against you is obedience to the Father. "For he bore the sin of many, and made intercession for the transgressors" (Isaiah 53:12b).

Let me clarify here that we don't bear other people's sins in order to provide them salvation—only Christ alone can make that claim. But we *are* called to "bear with each other and forgive one another if any of you has a grievance against someone. Forgive as the Lord forgave you" (Colossians 3:13).

Here's a few thoughts that have helped me in my own forgiveness process:

Forgiveness is releasing the debt that must be immediately rectified and giving it to the Lord to handle.

Forgiveness is releasing myself from the burdens I was never meant to carry.

Forgiveness is blocking the devil's attempts to implant heart rot: anger, bitterness, and revenge.

God will avenge, and he will repay in his timing.

He is a God who is patient and compassionate, but he is also a God of justice and peace.

One day, God will judge every word and deed, and no one gets off the hook.

I have to be vigilant over my own heart to make sure it's clean first.

I've got to trust his timing to settle the score in my life and in the lives of others.

I want to free myself from the devil's schemes to taint and tarnish my beautiful heart.

If I truly love the Lord, I must make the choice to obey his commands including the command to forgive.

I want to forgive so that God will forgive me. (Matthew 6:14)

◆

Writing letters of forgiveness to Patrick and Heidi, Jerry and Janet, and everyone else involved (ED's, Wilsons, Jacksons, Spencers, VP, head pastor, worship pastor, elders, etc.) was very healing for me. Part of the grief recovery exercise was to read them out loud to your partner. This verbalization allowed me to speak words I wasn't allowed or able to speak prior. It was a sacred moment offering forgiveness and releasing the debt to the Lord. It brought closure to these relationships and who I had hoped these people would be, say, and do.

Then there was the issue of hating myself. I suspect this is something many who have suffered recurring rejection, emotional neglect, or any kind of abuse struggle with. I had to forgive myself for what I didn't know at the time, how I could have been stronger back then, or how I could have spoken up in better ways at the right moments. I had to forgive myself for who I was before, what I didn't know, and how I handled the way we were being treated. I didn't know what I didn't know. I needed God's perspective of who I was and what my value was, not how others defined me. "I praise you because I am fearfully and wonderfully made; your works are wonderful, I know that full well" (Psalm 139:14).

There was also this issue of God. Did I trust God? I kept coming back to, *how could I dedicate my life to the Lord and it turn out like this?* I trusted God when I entered into this mission, and yet He allowed me to be wounded so deeply I didn't know up from down anymore. Could I trust him again? Would staying in ministry mean more of this level of suffering? I mean, I could always immerse myself in politics or get my real estate license instead. Any other secular job would be better than ministry, right?

Ultimately, I had made my choice years before. Jesus was all I had. He was everything to me, my life's purpose. Not fully understanding the *why* of our circumstances, I remembered my covenant agreement I made with God in February 2018. Come what may, I was his to use as he pleased. I had decided to follow Jesus, and there was no turning back for me. If this immense suffering was part of the process, then I had to accept that God was sovereign and all-knowing, and I was not. I wrote a forgiveness letter to God.

As time marched on, my mind began rightly dividing

between the men of God I trusted and God himself. Where these men once represented the ministry of the Lord in my life, I began to separate the character and nature of God vs. these men because of the fruit they exhibited. The Bible tells us God is "gracious and compassionate, slow to anger and rich in love" (Psalm 145:8). I could not attribute the sins of men claiming to represent God as a reflection of who God is. God and man are not one and the same, not even close. Men will sin and fall short. God never makes mistakes.

These delineations cause me to hold more firmly to God alone as my rock and my fortress, my Redeemer. Basing your trust in man is futile, for it doesn't take long before that foundation will be shaken and crumble to pieces. I've learned to trust in God alone as my anchor and source, and I've learned to keep men in their proper place. I'm no longer able to elevate man in my thinking because I know we as humans are all like grass, all sinful in nature, all in desperate need of a Savior. No good can come out of a man or woman of God unless Christ indeed lives inside of them, conquering sin in their heart. Only he is good (Matthew 19:17).

It took much time, talking, and tears to forgiveness, but the process was slowly moving forward. I felt an increased sense of peace over the situation. The intrusive thoughts and insomnia had gone away. The mental anguish and the heavy, physical weight that came along with it seemed to be lifting. I was on the road to recovery!

Near the end of winter, I began thinking about what

God was showing me through this experience. What did he want me to learn? What was I supposed to do with this information?

I thought about the fragile nature of the human heart. I knew how easily it was for mine to slowly and methodically become broken over time by life's bumps, bruises, and misfortunes. I thought about how I had really needed and wanted the people in charge of our family to truly love us, listen to us, and mentor us. I thought of other people who have been wounded by the Church.

A picture came into my mind of God caring for the broken-hearted. A few days later my kids came home from school and I ran across a single white sheet of computer paper laying on the back of our couch. On this paper was that very image, and I knew this was God's confirmation. God wants people to know that He sees the broken, the wounded, the sidelined, and the ones who never quite measured up to the 'system.' He never intended for it to be this way, but the result of sin in a fallen world produces undesirable outcomes. God is in the business of mending and healing hearts.

Making music was also part of my healing process. Even though I felt my singing had been rejected in college when I studied voice and then again by the Church, I began song writing as a means of expressing what had happened and what I truly believed. After the spiritual, mental, emotional, and relational abuse from the Agency and our local church leadership, I was a complete mess. I hated myself, and I had no desire to sing anymore. I had lost my voice. Again.

Regardless of these facts, I started getting the desire

to make music so I bought a used guitar and learned a few chords. Strumming was slow going. Between a world of rejection, a voice that had been cut off, and a battle-scarred heart, I sat, numb, on my living room couch and began to play the song "How Great is the Love" by Meredith Andrews.

At this time, I felt God was disappointed in me and the whole world had left me in my greatest time of need. I couldn't feel God. I wasn't sure he really loved me. I definitely didn't love myself. The lyrics to this song spoke truth to my heart bit by bit, breathing life into a lifeless situation. God's love never fails (1 Corinthians 13:8).

Weeks went by, and I picked up a little speed on the guitar. By this time, I had also moved to the piano in the next room since it was my stronger instrument of the two. I desired to do more. I asked God to please help me with my music. Over the next weeks and months, He inspired lyrics and melodies, and songs slowly came together. This was an important piece to my healing process as I sung about the hurt and brokenness, all the while reinstating my faith and trust in God even through the disappointments of life.

I would like to take a moment here to clarify something. While we are called to forgive the human person who caused offense, we are not called to overlook the devil's schemes to steal, kill, and destroy the seeds of faith in the hearts of men. Be on guard, "your enemy the devil prowls around like a roaring lion looking for someone to devour" (1 Peter 5:8).

Oftentimes, he will do this through the sins and offenses of people we trust. He especially likes to use leaders of Christian faith because he knows if one falls, chances are that individual's following may also become disillusioned and fall away from the faith as well. If it's possible, Satan might as well kill a hundred or a thousand sheep with one stone. If a leader has a foothold of sin, the devil will certainly use it to his advantage to wound and attempt to destroy the faith of the people around that person.

While we are called to love and pray for our brothers and sisters who offend us, we are not called as believers to cower before the spiritual Goliaths within the Church and be trampled by the enemy because we laid down our weapons out of "love" and "forgiveness." No, we do not love the devil or the curse of sin and its destruction. We are not called to stand idly by in toleration of sin.

I began to see past the people and remind myself there was a bigger battle at play. Identifying the real enemy is key. There is a spiritual battle, and we are called to wage warfare. "For our struggle is not against flesh and blood but against the rulers, against the authorities, against the powers of this dark world, and against the spiritual forces of evil in the heavenly realms" (Ephesians 6:12).

The devil wants your eyes focused on the person or people. He wants you to turn against God and blame him for the misdeeds of sinful men and the destructive results of living in a fallen, sinful world. He wants to trap you in the bitterness and anger of unforgiveness towards those around you. Lastly, Satan wants you to self-destruct through his lies of abandonment, betrayal, shame, self-condemnation, and a myriad of others. He will attack you mercilessly with temptation and get you to fall for fleshly appetites.

The devil doesn't play fair. He is crafty, cunning, and merciless. He will do all these things and more while staying hidden from sight. He blames everyone else, causing people to forget that he's actually the one behind it all. He's the one scheming and orchestrating the unfortunate, inopportune events of our lives in a broken world in order to turn humans against God, against each other, and against their very selves.

I'm calling Satan's bluff right now. His game is up. I'm no longer going to see things the way he wants me to see them. He's a liar. I'm not going to fall for the raging storms of life and the disillusionment the devil wants to bring through them. I know my God, and I stand on his Word that reveals God's true character and nature!

> "Therefore put on the full armor of God, so that when the day of evil comes, you may be able to stand your ground, and after you have done everything, to stand."
> Ephesians 6:13

CHAPTER 10

SUFFERING AND FAITH

Our minds are powerful things. When circumstances cross our paths that we don't like, don't want, or can't explain, our brains will work tirelessly until it finds a reasonable explanation. We desire to *know.* To explain the unexplainable. To solve the problem and fix things to our satisfaction. We don't like feeling ignorant, helpless, or out of control.

Suffering is one such thing many people have sought the reason, the answer, or the peaceful reconciliation regarding horrific happenstances. There's the issue of sin, pain, and injustice. Life is unfair. For some, life is inescapable suffering and grief. Thousands, if not millions, have asked the question: *Why?* Why God? Why me? Why this? Sometimes we search tirelessly or pray to God for the answers and are met with silence.

In the face of suffering, many become bitter at God and ultimately reject Him. When immediate relief or rescue or justice is not provided by an apparently all-powerful, all-knowing, all-seeing God, he must not be who he said he is. He must not see me. See my pain and provide rescue right *now*. We reason he must be absent, distant, unjust, unloving, powerless, heartless, or careless.

If you have been wounded by the Church, I feel your pain. People may fail you, cause you to suffer, or send you unheeded into the valley of the shadow of death. It seems bitterly unfair the pain others may have inflicted and the devastating ripple effects it may have left upon your day-to-day life or that of your family. If you have found yourself in this situation, let us take a moment to recall the examples of a few characters in the Bible who also suffered wrongdoing, rejection, and betrayal.

If anyone could complain about rejection and injustice, it was David. Running and hiding from Saul's jealous rage and assassination attempts, David knew one day he would be king, but didn't know how or when it would happen. He often wrote of his plight, his oppressors, his discouragement, and his weakness. He was at the mercy of men and God's timetable.

David couldn't yet see how the events of his life would ever straighten out, but he had his faith in God alone when he stated, "The Lord will fulfill his purpose for me" (Psalm 138:8). David wrote, "My flesh and my heart may fail, but God is the strength of my life and my portion forever" (Psalm 73:26). His psalms clearly depict his turmoil, but through it all, he resorted to giving glory and praise to God. His rock, solid faith and his heartfelt lyrics to unknown melodies minister to millions still today.

Remember Joseph, whose own brothers were so jealous, they threw him into a cistern intending to kill him. They ended up selling Joseph as a slave and feigning his death to their father. Joseph worked with integrity, faithfulness, and excellence for Potiphar in Egypt. Regardless, he found himself in yet another dank cell after a series of misrepresentations and a horrific betrayal by Potiphar's wife.

God never forgot Joseph when he was in yet another dark dungeon of despair although it may have certainly felt like God abandoned him again. God had a greater plan and purpose for Joseph's life. Just when he thought things would never change, the appointed time came, and God raised Joseph up to stand before Pharoah. God orchestrated the events of Joseph's life through the misdeeds, misrepresentations, chaos, and confusion inflicted upon his life by the failures of both men and women alike, yet he never resorted to blaming and cursing God. He patiently entrusted himself to the mighty hand and watchful eye of God.

Joseph could finally see God's bigger picture for his life many years later when God gave him wisdom to store up food for the nations because of a coming famine, becoming Pharoah's right-hand advisor. Joseph then saw the prophecies over his life come to fruition. He stated, "You intended to harm me, but God intended it for good to accomplish what is now being done, the saving of many lives" (Genesis 50:20).

If God has called you to be his servant, there may also be times your faith will be tested. God tested Abraham's devotion when he called upon Abraham to sacrifice his only son conceived by Sarah and heir to the promise, Isaac. Abraham obeyed even though it made absolutely no sense. God was pleased with Abraham's obedience, faith, and love for him above all else, and provided a ram instead (Genesis 22).

God tested Job's faith as well. Through a series of unfortunate events brought on by the devil *with the Lord's permission*, Job lost his crops, his flocks, and his children. Then his body was stricken with infirmity. Through it all, Job determined not to curse God, but rather stated, "Though he slay me, yet will I hope in him" (Job 13:15). God was pleased with Job's steadfast faith, the devil was proved wrong, and the Lord greatly blessed the latter part of Job's life. "As you know, we count as blessed those who have persevered. You have heard of Job's perseverance and have seen what the Lord finally brought about. The Lord is full of compassion and mercy" (James 5:11).

Finally, let us not forget the most important example and name above all names: Jesus. No human on earth can fully comprehend or describe the suffering of the Messiah. He bore the sins of the whole world, suffered, and died a brutal death.

> "He grew up before him like a tender shoot, and like a root out of dry ground. He had no beauty or majesty to attract us to him, nothing in his appearance that we should desire him. He was despised and rejected by mankind, a man of suffering, and familiar with pain. Like one from whom people hide their faces he was despised, and we held him in low esteem." Isaiah 53:2–3

Jesus was the perfect sacrifice, a lamb without spot, wrinkle, or blemish. He came to bear the weight of our sin though he did no wrong. He entrusted himself to his Father and was obedient even to death, offering himself for all mankind: past, present, and future. For you. For me.

This is the greatest love story ever told, and it has been told millions of times. It will continue to be told. The entire Bible revolves around this beautiful love story of how God loved his created humans so much, he chose to make the ultimate sacrifice of *his very Son* in order to bring salvation. All of history hinges upon this event.

What other god can make this claim? What other god has demonstrated this kind of love? There is none. Where other gods demand sacrifice, service, blood, and appeasement—or face wrath—God shed his *own* blood on behalf of all mankind from the beginning of time until now. There is not one ounce of love in the gods of this world. The full embodiment of love was found only in the person of Jesus Christ: God's offering to his beloved creation for salvation from sin and death. There is no other god like Him. "Greater love has no one than this: to lay down one's life for one's friends" (John 15:13).

Let us not forget the example of Jesus as a model for his disciples. The religious elite of his day rejected him and poured out abuses upon him, yet he chose to forgive them and pray for them in the middle of his intense suffering and death on the cross. "Jesus said, 'Father, forgive them, for they know not what they are doing'" (Luke 23:34).

If you have also sustained significant injury from fellow believers or from those who were supposed to champion you, I'd like to encourage you. You may feel like those people threw you into a fiery furnace and everything in your world is wrong right now. I understand.

Turn your eyes toward Jesus and away from those people for a moment. Jesus is standing there in the fire with you, arms open wide with scars in his hands. He's never left you. You can trust him to show you many things as he was faithful to instruct the two disciples he met while walking the road to Emmaus.

If you will turn your gaze toward Jesus, he may show you some things as I have also come to learn by sitting still and resting by quiet waters for quite some time. While we can never fully know the mind of God or explain his ways, the circumstances you've found yourself in may have several purposes. Let's take a look at a few nuggets I've grasped that could be true of your situation as well.

Gold nuggets of faith from the fiery furnace of suffering:

You may be in a great contest of your faith.

The devil is eager for you to fail.

God is waiting to see if your faith proves as gold.

God is working patience and endurance into your character.

God may be revealing those around you with mixed motives and impure hearts.

God may be removing certain compromised individuals from your life.

God may be realigning you with others who are meant to run alongside you.

God has seen and will hold others accountable in the end.

God has something better prepared for you.

God will bring beauty from ashes, joy from mourning, and praise from despair. (Isaiah 61:3)

God wants to pull you aside for a season to rest by crystal waters. (Psalm 23:2)

God wants to speak truth to your heart and mind.

God wants to heal you of any lingering wounds from earlier in your life that may trip you up in the future.

God wants to use the battle to strengthen and equip you.

God is molding you into a stronger soldier for Christ.

God will take what the devil meant for evil and turn it around for your benefit.

You'll be stronger and more equipped to recognize the devil's tactics in the future.

God will use you to help comfort and encourage others along the same path.

God may be forming in you a heart of compassion and empathy to identify with those who suffer.

God will use this trial to mold your character into that of Christ's.

Those who suffer with Christ can consider themselves blessed by God.

God will use this to drive your faith deeper in him than it's ever been before.

God is faithful and his mercies and compassion are new each morning. (Lamentations 3:22-24)

God will deliver you from the fire and may choose to bless or promote you if you've stood the test.

The Holy Spirit who lives in you will bring you out victorious in God's perfect timing if you stand firm.

Through your suffering, Jesus will receive the honor and glory and praise due his name.

God will have any myriad of other purposes for your suffering that I won't be able to identify or explain.

If the circumstances of your life have buried you underground, take heart. God is not finished with you yet! You may be in a time of hiding where God has planted you as a seed in depths of darkness in order for your roots to grow before sprouts will burst forth into daylight. Just as a butterfly spends time inside its cocoon, God may be drawing you aside into a season of hiddenness and preparation with him in order to do a deep transformative work inside of you before He's ready to release you and let you fly! "Let perseverance finish its work so that you may be mature and complete, not lacking anything." James 1:4

I believe God has a special grace for people in the fire, so give yourself some too. We are human, and we mess up. God knows the weaknesses and temptations common to man because Jesus was a man himself. Although he never sinned, we humans stumble and fall. Sometimes it takes us a lot longer to learn or hear the Lord than we think it should take. What we think should come naturally or quickly might actually need quite a bit more time to fully come around.

Even Peter faltered when the Lord invited him out of the boat and onto the water. Peter's faith failed, and he began to sink. It's never too late for you or for me. If you've found yourself sinking but want to be saved, that's when Jesus steps in with a helping hand. It's okay to recognize that there's times when we simply can't do it on our own. Cry out to God and reach out your hand, and he will grab ahold of you.

Ultimately, I've had to comfort myself with the fact that with the proper perspective, God uses suffering, pain, and injustice to conform a chosen people into the image and likeness of his Son. "For those God foreknew he also predestined to be conformed to the image of his Son, that he might be the firstborn among many brothers and sisters" (Romans 8:29). Although it may baffle human reasoning, we can rejoice in persecution and trials. "The apostles left the Sanhedrin, rejoicing because they had been counted worthy of suffering disgrace for the Name" (Acts 5:41).

God wants to purify and purge his people of love for this world and its idolatries, not to fulfill worldly desires and passionate lusts of the flesh. Often this sanctification process happens *through* suffering. "Therefore, since Christ suffered in his body, arm yourselves also with the same attitude, because whoever suffers in the body is done with sin" (1 Peter 4:1).

Today, some leaders present Christianity as a path to money, power, possessions, and prosperity. Don't buy it. God is not a vending machine to satisfy earthly cravings nor is he a puppet. He warns his people not to love this world or the things of this world (1 John 2:15). "For the love of money is a root of all kinds of evil. Some people, eager for money, have wandered from the faith and pierced themselves with many griefs" (1 Timothy 6:10).

Don't become disillusioned with God by the pain of suffering to the point of walking away from the faith. While having to endure the fiery furnace, a person's entire being vigilantly pleads for deliverance or rescue! We are all human.

Suffering never feels good, it's never convenient, and it's the last thing we desire for our lives. It's the path no one asked for and no person in their right mind would naturally choose. "No discipline seems pleasant at the time, but painful. Later on, however, it produces a harvest of righteousness and peace for those who have been trained by it" (Hebrews 12:11).

Suffering is *meant* to be uncomfortable because the people of God are not *meant* to live for the things of this world, but rather, for things of eternity.

> "Praise be to the God and Father of our Lord Jesus Christ! In his great mercy he has given us new birth into a living hope through the resurrection of Jesus Christ from the dead, and into an inheritance that can never perish, spoil or fade. This inheritance is kept in heaven for you, who through faith are shielded by God's power until the coming of the salvation that is ready to be revealed in the last time. In all this you greatly rejoice, though now for a little while you may have had to suffer grief in all kinds of trials. These have come so that the proven genuineness of your faith—of greater worth than gold, which perishes even though refined by fire—may result in praise, glory, and honor when Jesus Christ is revealed." 1 Peter 1:3-7

If the circumstances of your life have driven you to your knees, and you have found yourself in the valley of the shadow of death, hold tight and don't give up on your faith in God! Look to the examples of other men and women in the Bible, and let their stories encourage you. Grab ahold of God's Word, hide yourself in God for a season, stand firm, and watch and see what the Lord will do in your life. Hallelujah!

> "My son, do not despise the Lord's discipline, and do not resent his rebuke, because the Lord disciplines those he loves, as a father the son he delights in." Proverbs 3:11-12

> "'For my thoughts are not your thoughts, neither are your ways my ways,' declares the Lord." Isaiah 55:8

> "Praise be to the God and Father of our Lord Jesus Christ, the Father of compassion and the God of all comfort, who comforts us in all our troubles, so that we can comfort those in any trouble with the comfort we ourselves receive from God." 2 Corinthians 1:3-4

CHAPTER 11

SUPPRESSED ARISING

Putting the past behind and leaving it at the foot of the cross, it was easier to dream again. New ideas, new partnerships, and new options! We received verbal commitment from the assistant pastor the previous summer that our new church fellowship would send us again if the Lord was calling us to return overseas (one of the reasons why we had selected to attend this fellowship during our time of healing).

With this in mind and much of the healing process behind us, Chad and I developed a new vision with our national partners from the field, created an official proposal, and met with the assistant pastor in April. We communicated we were ready to discuss our family's return to the field with the understanding they would become our sending church. We handed him a copy of our proposal.

The next day, we emailed our official mission proposal to him, of which he had promised to forward on to the elders. We waited several weeks in May with no response or acknowledgment of receipt from the church elders. Weeks went by and the silence became not only deafening, but also discouraging.

Chad had simultaneously applied and been accepted to teach at the international Christian school. The school was waiting to hear back from us about coming before the start of the next school year. Setting up our household would have been easy, requiring only a single-day shift to its destination.

Over the course of the next few months, we continued meeting with the assistant pastor with hard copies of information and emailed two more letters of intent of which he promised to forward to the elders. Chad reached out to one of his elder friends in June and was surprised to learn he had never seen any letter regarding our family. As time slipped by, our window of opportunity to shift back to the field before the coming school year became out of reach. Summer plans filled in with family, and we were booked.

Chad and I made a final determination in July that our mission must have a dead end if there's no sending church. We arranged one final trip to the field for August to visit our friends and handle our household that had been in storage before the start of our school year in the States. Two and a half years has elapsed since our evacuation.

Uncertain what it would feel like to return to this particular field, we were surprised with how it seemed like yesterday since we'd been there. It was almost like we never left. Culture wasn't shocking, and it wasn't long before we had our vehicle and were driving all over town—shifting our furniture and boxes from the warehouse to our friend's home in order to sort, pack, donate, and disperse belongings. However, our friends were only able to accept half the furniture because their flat was smaller than our previous one. This left the other half of our household still in storage.

We shared many laughs and wonderful meals together that week. We helped them set up their new ministry house and transferred furniture, supplies, and vehicle for their use. We kept in discussion a continued partnership with these humble and sweet yet spunky national partners. We met the international school principal and toured their new campus. This trip was largely healing for me and provided hope for a new future despite the ashes of the first partnership we had on that particular field.

When we arrived home, we attended our new church the next Sunday morning. An elder opened the service in prayer. The entire church proceeded to pray for another couple who was currently on a STMT in a neighboring Asian country to our field. I was saddened because I knew the church had not corporately prayed for us on Sunday morning while we were in Asia the previous week, even though we had submitted a written request they do so. I sat looking around the church body knowing these people had no clue we had just been around the world and back on a STMT.

We met with the associate pastor again to debrief our trip. It was in this meeting that we continued to share our vision and handed him a fourth print-out explaining the different pieces. I again asked if the mission department team and the elders could please be praying about sending us. Surprisingly, the associate pastor said, "We don't like it when people come into the church with their vision and try to manipulate the pastors into following their wishes."

His comment startled me. I had to process his statement later because it really rubbed me the wrong way. I actually felt we were the ones being manipulated to attend this fellowship in the first place with his promise to send us the previous summer, and then no corresponding follow through when we communicated it was time.

I met with the head pastor's wife to share my frustration over the associate pastor's comment, and her response was we had to "earn the right" to be sent by this church. I told her Chad had met with the associate pastor a year prior in which he verbally committed to sending our family once we were healed. She replied, "He had no right to say that."

We had also been under the teaching of her husband, the head pastor, at our original home church for about 12 years, serving faithfully in a variety of ministry departments. I mentioned our lengthy track record at their previous church. She said, "None of that counts for anything, and you have to prove yourselves at this new church plant."

I then wondered how the women's ministry director got her position at the new church plant if she had no track record to lean on from their former church? She had been a leader in women's ministry there for many years. Did that count for something when they selected her? I felt it was a double standard.

I shared we felt the Lord directing our family into missions and serving in the mission department. Chad had been volunteering his time by attending every single "mission commission" meeting and then working at home to help create their founding documents. I explained this is why I turned down a role in their women's ministry, and she said, "Wrong answer."

I continued to share our vision of inviting our Asian friends, our new national partners, to the church to present their ministry and raise support, and she said, "On whose authority are you bringing these people into our church?" I replied, "If Chad and I are partnering with them." She shook her head in firm disapproval.

She challenged me by asking who we were in relationship with at the church, and I said there were so many people there from our former church that we've known for many years. There were also other families who had known Chad through his music educator role in our community. This did not satisfy her.

Finally, she said, "You know I'm for you, right?" Feeling completely shut down, I left that meeting and went home. I had to process yet again the church leadership that was presenting itself to our family.

Not one pastor or elder of the church had met with us to discuss our mission experience or pray over us, even after we had sent them a letter early on communicating our hurt over what transpired and our purpose to heal within their community. They were having the opposite effect on us and perpetuating the pattern of feelings of neglect and rejection. Correct me if I'm wrong, but I believe a reasonable expectation from someone with the title "pastor" is that they are pastoral in nature.

I then thought about the activities of this particular church and its elders. Why hadn't any of the elders responded to our communications? Chad asked an elder friend if he'd seen our letters, and the answer was *no*. If they were too busy to meet with us, what had been their recent focus?

Over the last three to four months, this church body received almost weekly updates on the sale and purchase of the neighboring one-third acre. This church wanted to buy it in order to expand their parking lot. Earlier, the church poured money into new chairs, technology, light fixtures, and paint. There is also an architectural plan for an addition to the building.

Given four months and four letters with no response from the elders, their priority of remodeling the building and expanding their parking lot, and being shut down by the head pastor's wife at every turn, we determined the Lord had closed that door as well. We sent a letter to the pastor we had been meeting with to communicate our departure.

He called Chad and asked why leaving would help us. He was meant to shepherd us. We thought to ourselves, *over the course of the last year, how had we been shepherded*?

CHAPTER 12

MAINSTREAM CHRISTIANITY

We're going to switch gears and begin addressing the hierarchical, religious, political structure that has become part of the Church. Let's remember that Jesus didn't filter his language when addressing the religious elite of his day. His pointed language offended these men which only angered them further. They didn't like being challenged or called into question, and they often sought to trap Jesus in his words or eliminate him entirely. This only revealed the hardness of their hearts.

We, maybe like you, are asking the question: who will shepherd our family? How will the church leadership spend time with us or get to know us? Who will provide Godly counsel in an honoring mentorship? Who will encourage and support our calling rather than make us fit into their mold? We feel so alone, and I know we're not the only sheep who feel utterly lost right now. Perhaps there are others like us wandering from one sheep fold to the next, looking for a shepherd.

My guess is this may be more of a normal occurrence within churches. Apparently, submission to current authority is a must, even if they don't hold discussions with you, don't provide a compassionate shepherd, and aren't really making any effort to get to know your family. However, they want you to volunteer your service and your money.

It appears to me like subjection to pastors and their elder puppets is required so they can retain charge of the people, charge of the vision, and charge of the money. Do elders feel like they can challenge the 'man of the house'—the head pastor with the seminary degree? Were we allowed to challenge?

In the example of our new fellowship, the people are being led to sign official "membership," meant to commit their regular attendance, service, and finances to this particular house of God. They will give their tithe, and that building's coffers will grow.

While none of these things are outright wrong, I would like to communicate my hesitancy. As I mentioned above, the church's focus for the last three to four months had been on purchasing a neighboring sliver of property for $150,000 cash in order to expand their parking lot. The elders and members voted to send that money, literally, right into the ground. They also just voted and approved a $500,000 remodel project. Apparently, it's more important that patrons can park and sit comfortably as they come to attend Sunday morning service than to develop the vision and mission to reach lost souls in poverty-stricken areas of gospel-destitute Asia. Anything to keep them coming, I guess. First world problems.

Can I please share that I think nothing could be further from the heart of God? I've lived in a third world country, and it grieves my heart to see the American Church's money deterred from local or global mission fields by such projects. I've seen the dire need of the poor as some of you may have probably seen as well. Some people don't even know where their next meal is coming from.

Does the Church allocate 10% of their budget to their missions department and 90% stays inhouse? Someone please explain, I really don't know. "If anyone has material possessions and sees a brother or sister in need but has no pity on them, how can the love of God be in that person?" (1 John 3:17).

Men of God, I implore you. God's heart is not in a building or a parking lot. God's heart is with the poor and with the broken, lost people of the world. God loves the people of the world. Please, can the church's money go to unreached souls, the naked, hungry, and hurting? Why does the church's money have to go to building remodels and parking lots? Where is the priority?

Additionally, I see a large collective of American pastors who have turned their position in the church into a career. How many millions of dollars across the country are going into the pockets of pastors and staff? I guess a pastor could argue "the hardworking farmer should be the first to receive a share of the crops" (2 Timothy 2:6). But to what extent?

What are the pastor and staff salaries? What do the retirement funds coming out of the Church look like? It was also Paul that said, "But if we have food and clothing, we will be content with that" (1 Timothy 6:8).

I'm not saying a pastor shouldn't be compensated for

his work. I know pastors are working, but so are many others as they volunteer their service on any given week. I'm just saying if the Church staff are absorbing much of the income, how are we as a body doing in performing the real duties of the Church?

Why can't we alter career pastor/staff salaries and retirement funds in order to provide for the needy and bring in a harvest? Is anyone willing to sell house or land from time to time to contribute to those in need (Acts 4:34)? Who will step forward and lead by example? "Your gold and silver are corroded. Their corrosion will testify against you and eat your flesh like fire. You have hoarded wealth in the last days" (James 5:3).

Finally, members are expected to plug in and serve this gathering of believers in one of the departments of the church. While serving your local church gathering is wonderful and necessary, here's my question. If all believers only serve their local gathering, who is actually doing the work of reaching the lost?

Are the leaders directing the people to serve only their body, keeping them close at hand, mainly providing attractive in-house ministries to draw additional consumers to their building? Or are people being trained and encouraged to do the work of the Church by reaching their neighborhoods and cities with the love of God? It might be time to take into consideration the actual activities and actions of being a disciple of Christ and take inventory of your fellowship to see if pastors are not only "making disciples" but also "teaching them to obey" the Lord's commands (see Matthew 28:18-20).

Let's be aware of the way in which the mainstream

American Christian Church is building. Let's be very careful where money is going because this reflects the state of our hearts. If the majority of the Lord's money is going into pastor/staff pockets or temporal, material buildings while poverty-stricken, gospel-destitute people are dying every day, maybe it's time to take a quick heart examination. Let's assess if the Church is investing in human beings at the core of the Lord's heart. Are the leader's hearts clean?

Perhaps one reason the Church has declined into a very weak state today is because sin is not being dealt with appropriately amongst leadership. If the hearts of leaders are not clean, how can the blind lead? "Leave them; they are blind guides. If the blind lead the blind, both will fall into a pit" (Matthew 15:14).

I believe we as a church have not been perfected in love. I believe sin still exists in the hearts of God's men and women. The result is people in leadership may be unknowingly usurping the throne and will of God and the Lord's money to build earthly structures upon their own pleasure and wishes for growing a Church as a local business for the glory of man. Again, this may not apply to every local gathering, but I want to present my heart's desire and ask thought-provoking questions. Some of you may have thought these same things. Others can come to their own conclusions.

Another reason why I think the Church has declined is because through tolerating sin they can no longer discern their enemy the devil. The Church has misdiagnosed the nature of the beast. We do not bow to the tyranny of the enemy within, thinking all sheep are sheep and one must love all and forgive all. No, we do not "obey our authorities" or church leaders if they are committing horrendous acts of treason against the Lord's sheep or the will of God. They are not sheep, but wolves in disguise.

Pastors should not say: "As far as it depends on you live at peace with everyone" (Romans 12:18), and then require forgiveness from the abused while the devourer runs off to find their next target. This is absurd! The devil is waging war on the Church, and his emissaries are cleverly disguised within. This is not a time to lay down in safety, rest, and peace! This is a time of war! "A time to love and a time to hate, a time for war and a time for peace" (Ecclesiastes 3:8).

We do not live at peace with sin or the devil operating through so-called "pastors." Remember, the manipulator will always require the other person to forgive and live at peace with them, never taking any responsibility for their own sin, but rather heaping abuses on everyone else and gaslighting the situation, calling it one thing when it's actually the other. Unfortunately, the abuser won't change unless accountability for sin comes into play by fellow leaders of church office. Sin must be dealt with amongst leadership in order to keep the body pure and functioning healthily.

In addition, some church pastors may be misdiagnosing the spiritual hour in which we live. Is it possible that teaching pastors in pulpits across the country are preaching the same old sermons with no added alarm regarding the sign of the times? Could it be that pastors aren't really wanting to preach truth in case it ruffles feathers and causes people to leave as their money also walks out the door? Perhaps these men and women know the slander and lies swirling within the heart of the Church behind closed doors and find no need to upset the apple cart? After all, their salary might be at stake. People might walk out and the organization collapse, so it's best not to say anything at all, right?

The Church has not only compromised by tolerating sin, laying down her weapons of warfare, and preaching "peace" in a time of "war," but she has also allowed worldly mixture into the body. Systems of the world have crept into the church meant to be set apart. How will the Church's light shine in a dark world if we look the same?

Mainstream American churches today have become a masterful showcase of American Idol proportions. These attractive productions catch the fancy of the everyday religious churchgoer, displaying only the best and brightest by worldly standards, and filling the church's pockets with funds to pay the main characters and perfect their theater. It's big business.

These pastors preach "grace, grace" but deliver a half-truth. Attendees are taught just by believing that Jesus died on the cross and rose again, giving tithe, and coming on a Sunday to serve that they are saved and can live just like the world. In living no different from the world, then they are to expect to inherit God's kingdom of eternal life. "My people are destroyed from lack of knowledge" (Hosea 4:6).

By these messages, God's people are essentially given permission to live with idols remaining in their hearts. God is not interested in people's tithe or lip service during "worship" if their hearts are far from him (Matthew 15:18). The Bible clearly states what happens to idolaters.

I'm going to eliminate all the time and work it would take me to outline Scripture on sin, repentance, holiness, obedience, and fruit in this book. That would require an entire separate book. It's up to each individual to read the Word and come to their own conclusion what the New Testament even conveys about these things and how they relate to grace, salvation, and the difference between the knowledge *of* Christ and being *in* Christ.

> "Therefore let us move beyond the elementary teachings about Christ and be taken forward to maturity, not laying again the foundation of repentance from acts that lead to death, and of faith in God, instruction about baptisms, the laying on of hands, the resurrection of the dead, and eternal judgment" (Hebrews 6:1-2).

Let's not deceive ourselves or let the pastor water down the gospel. To eliminate the message of repentance and God's standards of holiness and obedience creates a weak, lackadaisical Church who allows the cancers of sin to devastate the body because they've already been saved by grace and can never be snatched away because God loves them.

God will judge our hearts, and he is not deceived merely by lip service or outward religious rituals. Jesus says many times that those who love him will obey (John 14:23). "Not everyone who says to me, 'Lord, Lord,' will enter the kingdom of heaven, but only the one who does the will of my Father who is in heaven" (Matthew 7:21).

Do we only have to "believe" that Jesus is who he is and continue on with life as normal, living for the pleasures of the world and looking just the same? Even the demons believe (James 2:19). Grace without truth is a counterfeit message just as faith without works is dead (James 2:26). Head knowledge without heart change is futile. "He will punish those who do not know God and do not obey the gospel of our Lord Jesus" (2 Thessalonians 1:8).

Be very careful, the message of grace alone while leaving room for sin to remain provides a license for idolatry. "This is the verdict: Light has come into the world, but people loved darkness instead of light because their deeds were evil" (John 3:19). "The wrath of God is being revealed from heaven against all the godlessness and wickedness of people, who suppress the truth by their wickedness" (Romans 1:18).

Yes, sin is pleasurable for a time but ultimately leads to destruction. God loves his treasured people too much to passively allow sin. Love does not ignore or give excuses for sin. Love aims to eradicate sin because sin leads to death. That is true love. Similarly, a loving parent will set rules and boundaries for their children in order to protect them from destruction. "The Lord disciplines the one he loves, and he chastens everyone he accepts as his son" (Hebrews 12:6).

Grace without truth only serves to appease the masses while they're deceptively walking a wide path straight to hell. It is a death sentence. Will the Noah's of today please stand up and start preaching righteousness and right standing with God? "Enter through the narrow gate. For wide is the gate and broad is the road that leads to destruction, and many enter through it. But small is the gate and narrow the road that leads to life, and only a few find it" (Matthew 7:13-14).

Furthermore, these teaching pastors think they can ignore the entirety of Scripture and preach only the messages of their choosing to their liking. They deny the power and working of the Holy Spirit. They erase his gifts. They scoff at those who pray in tongues. They reject the prophets, healing for today, baptism or outpouring of the Holy Spirit, amongst other things.

Not that we primarily seek manifestations or accept fleshly or demonic manifestations, but we desire only what is truly from the Holy Spirit in order to confirm the word of the Gospel. Ongoing discernment and testing of the spirits is needed. However, these men teach only what they want from Scripture while casting down what they don't like and can't control, rejecting and blaspheming the Holy Spirit.

> "But these people blaspheme in matters they do not understand. They are like unreasoning animals, creatures of instinct, born only to be caught and destroyed, and like animals they too will perish" (2 Peter 2:12).

> "Yet these people slander whatever they do not understand, and the very things they do understand by instinct—as irrational animals do—will destroy them" (Jude 1:10).

> "And so I tell you, every kind of sin and slander can be forgiven, but blasphemy against the Spirit will not be forgiven" (Matthew 12:31).

Meanwhile, the Spirit of the Living God is far from these establishments. He's been pushed out of these gatherings long ago. "Playing church" is an empty, religious activity devoid of any real meaning or relationship with God.

The songs of praise and worship emanating from these platforms are meaningless performances, and the microphone is vacant of any real value or power to save. The "church" building has either become a great hall or a social club with no real conviction, heart change, or salvation. It's merely theatricals, and the attendees pay for their tickets through their tithe, only to come enjoy next week's playwrights.

Finally, I think many in church leadership have lost the art of mentoring, partnering, and leading from a place of humility rather than lordship (1 Peter 5:3). I believe church leadership has lost the art of stewardship and humble servanthood. Are they listening to the people? Are they giving the mission or vision God has given others room to grow? Are they providing the necessary support for believers to be enlarged, engaged, and equipped within the family of God?

Let's not allow the church to revolve around a few good men and their need to control and build their earthly structure to display themselves. The political games happening in the church are a stench. Let's locate humble shepherds who truly have the Lord at heart, who preach both truth and grace, who stand on the whole of Scripture, who leave room for the Holy Spirit's workings, who protect and feed their sheep from a place of complete love and humility, who give to the poor and needy, and who build up the body by allowing their sheep to discover and utilize their spiritual gifts.

Let's find shepherds intent on equipping their people into good works, helping them flourish rather than stifling and suppressing the mission and vision God's given to his people because their own needs aren't being met first. The Church is greatly hindered by men who surround themselves only with people who comply with their every word, who play into the 'system,' or do and say only what their tickling ears want to hear.

We've been fed a series of half-truths from the pulpits across this nation resulting in a weakened Church who no longer knows who they are or what they're supposed to be doing in the earth today. We've narrowed in on some of the ways the devil has crept into the heart of the Church causing mass deception, division, and devastation.

There are many in the Church today who sense the urgency of the hour and the desperate need for change. We're not here to play games anymore. We're not here to preach a weak message and deny the power of an all-powerful God. The devil's had his way for far too long. Put your seatbelts on and hold onto your hats because this wild ride isn't over! We're in a spiritual war, and we're zeroing in on the target! Sharpen your swords, Church! All hands on deck!

"How can you say, 'We are wise, for we have the law of the Lord,' when actually the lying pen of the scribes has handled it falsely? The wise will be put to shame; they will be dismayed and trapped. Since they have rejected the word of the Lord, what kind of wisdom do they have? Therefore I will give their wives to other men and their fields to new owners. From the least to the greatest, all are greedy for gain; prophets and priests alike, all practice deceit. They dress the wound of my people as though it were not serious. 'Peace, peace,' they say, when there is no peace. Are they ashamed of their detestable conduct? No, they have no shame at all; they do not even know how to blush. So they will fall among the fallen; they will be brought down when they are punished, says the Lord.

Since my people are crushed, I am crushed; I mourn, and horror grips me. Is there no balm in Gilead? Is there no physician there? Why then is there no healing for the wound of my people?"

Jeremiah 8:8-12, 21-22

CHAPTER 13

"THE SYSTEM"

"There are six things the Lord hates, seven that are detestable to him: haughty eyes, a lying tongue, hands that shed innocent blood, a heart that devises wicked schemes, feet that are quick to rush into evil, a false witness who pours out lies and a person who stirs up conflict in the community." Proverbs 6:16-19

Many may have noticed in recent days there's a great exposure of corruption going on in the political, social, and business realm of the United States of America. The heart of God today desires to shine light on corruption within the spiritually "high places" of his Church as well in order to make amends. In fact, the physical world may, in part, reveal what is happening in the spiritual realm. If there's treason within our own nation's governmental institutions meant to steward, feed, and protect the people, perhaps this is also a reflection of the activities happening within the government of God's Church.

A couple years ago, God brought me to read Ezekiel 8 in which Ezekiel is provided an inside look at idolatrous men within temple walls. Similarly, I believe God wants to show his people *there is still sin in the hearts of his people*, and it begins at the "top." God sees the heart, and there is no hiding from God. He sees the idols of one's heart and the motives behind actions whether it be pride, money, fame, praises of man, ministry, or systems of this world that have crept into the Church. In his kindness, God will reveal to men their sin in order to lead them to repentance rather than destruction (Romans 2:4).

God is greatly grieved for his people, the sheep of his pasture. God sees the idolatry in his house. Like we read in Ezekiel's vision, wickedness is not stemming from the sheep. It's coming from leadership within the walls of the temple. I believe God's heart is grieving and wants to call attention to "wolves in sheep's clothing" running rampant inside church and religious organizational walls, placing their own needs first, devouring sheep, and jumping folds to prey upon the next. It's an atrocity in the Lord's house that must be dealt with. Let's take a look at how these wolves operate inside these organizations.

These organizations operate in self-preservation mode, serving the interests of the institution rather than treating their members like brothers and sisters in the house of the Lord. If anyone stands up as a "whistleblower" to address conflict or compromise that could threaten another's money, position, or reputation, that individual should expect vengeful attack until they are completely eliminated.

This happens quietly and stealthily through a series of lies and slander that might sound reasonable to the casual bystander who doesn't know the full story. The real reason for departures or resignations from these establishments happen unbeknownst to the general public so as not to alarm, otherwise it would expose the elite's demand for complete compliance from their puppets—else they suffer severe punishment or merciless reputational destruction.

After all, why not choose the lesser of two evils? The institution doesn't want to lose their 10% earnings from the missionary account that has been active for well over a decade containing handfuls of churches and individuals—versus the new missionary family supported by one church and a few family members and friends. Of course, the institution will do whatever is necessary to keep the larger account no matter the serious decline in spiritual health of the veteran.

Can I ask some serious questions here? Since when is the Church supposed to become institutionalized? What kind of governing model are they practicing? Could it possibly be a worldly model rather than the model given by Christ for his Church? Do ministers understand the ugly politics within this system are deterring people from wanting to enter into ministry?

Here's another question: At what point in our personal experience did the Agency actually support our family? On the flip side, they were probably happy to receive 10% of donations our family brought in. Just imagine what that number would be if there were dozens, hundreds, or even a thousand missionary accounts! They'd be rolling in the dough.

These big Agency oligarchs are sitting pretty in a beautiful white mansion on the top of a green, grassy hill and living the good life. This is not a figure of speech. This is literal. They even have a world-class chef cooking their meals!

How are these men and women actually serving the Lord, or are they mooching off the people who are sacrificing, serving, and facing all kinds of challenges on the ground in far reaches of the earth? Do these people truly represent the missionary family, or do they represent themselves? It's a clown circus if you ask me! They are the ones behind these "missionary graveyards!"

Let me tell you how these men are operating. The guilty paint themselves as innocent in a series of misrepresentations or lies. They even twist the truth, gaslighting the innocent and bending entire situations backwards in their favor. They often present themselves as the victim and the innocent as unstable or unfit for service. They do all they can to keep the truthteller from taking the witness stand. There's a lot of talk going on behind and around the witness, but never involving the witness. It's crafty and debilitating.

Nothing could be further from the truth or the heart of God. Nothing is hidden from his sight. He hears the slanderous words streaming from these spineless men's mouths behind closed doors as poison from a viper's bite, resulting in the slaughter of innocent blood.

"Everyone who does evil hates the light, and will not come into the light for fear that their deeds will be exposed." John 3:20

In regard to the national pastor on the field we were

serving, his spiritual decline was greatly apparent. He threatens the work of the gospel and hinders the reputation of Christ in that city. Others are like this too.

They belittle their sheep with their words—accusing them for the very things of which they are guilty—in order to keep others small and make themselves feel greater and more important. They collaborate with each other to manipulate and control people into subjection— or suffer punishment. They will cross healthy boundaries and come in between marriages. They don't want rules or expectations defined because they want them placed upon other's backs. They will abuse the Lord's money in secret, hoarding resources meant for others. These squanderers live off the church's funds meant to meet the needs of the hungry, naked, and unreached in the far corners of the earth. These are the pastors.

"Woe to them! They have taken the way of Cain; they have rushed for profit into Balaam's error; they have been destroyed in Korah's rebellion." Jude 1:11

God sees the sabotage and treason happening in his house, and he is greatly grieved at these atrocities that are coming from hypocritical, religious men in power. Men who, from a distance, appear to have the Lord's interests at heart in teaching God's Word or spreading the gospel. From all appearance, their words sound spiritual and their attitude seems humble. Do not be deceived. When you are lured into their inner circle and get muddled with them, you will be devoured. I am only one of many who have been slain.

I believe the Lord sent me into the lion's lair so I would learn, I would see, and I would personally experience the deep betrayal and grievances that are going on in the house of God! I'm speaking up for those who have not. I'm desperately crying, "Wolf!" Can anyone hear me? Does anyone understand? This is not a joke, and this is not an exercise. This is reality.

The hearts of these men are not honorable nor clean. They perform wicked deeds against the innocent in order to preserve their own ministries and all that brings to them: money, supporters, positions, sparkling reputations, and charming personalities. They will not stop at anything if someone rises with any testimony challenging their character or authority. These oppressors gaslight these individuals and misrepresent factual truths in order to make the innocent appear guilty. The abused, trying to expose the problems in order to repair that which is broken, will be punished and terminated. *Nothing is as it seems.*

"In fact, everyone who wants to live a godly life in Christ Jesus will be persecuted, while evildoers and imposters will go from bad to worse, deceiving and being deceived." 2 Timothy 3:12

Matthew 18 is key and must be practiced—the very thing we were accused of not doing. In our situation, we addressed the individual, then we engaged the next level of leadership, then the next level of leadership, then finally the top level within the Agency. Same process within our church. We addressed the individual, then engaged the executive pastor, then the head pastor and worship arts pastor, then finally the elders.

If the VP of the Agency and the elders of our church all did not engage the sinner, how will the Church ever clean house? Are all these men so fixed upon their own reputations, the placating for others' approval, the stroking of egos, and the mismanagement of funds, that they're too afraid to call each other's sin to account? Or are they being fed lies by those around them?

This collaboration with evil leaves the sheep of the pasture open for the wolf's next meal, sorry to say. It's a devastating fate and a dire situation. If you're in leadership and you let these things slip by unaddressed, you've become a pacifist and a participant in the eager wolves' open season and vicious appetite. It's an all-out war on God's people, and the enemy is within!

> "These people are blemishes at your love feasts, eating with you without the slightest qualm—shepherds who feed only themselves. They are clouds without rain, blown along by the wind; autumn trees, without fruit and uprooted—twice dead." Jude 1:12

The sinner must be expected to listen to the individual they have sinned against. It doesn't matter what title or position they claim; we are all brothers and sisters in the house of God. No one should consider himself "above reproach," for if they claim they have no sin, they only deceive themselves (1 John 1:8).

If they won't listen, then take another with you for the testimony of two or three witnesses. If they still won't listen, take them before the church (pastoral or elder or mission boards). If they choose not to listen nor repent even before the Church, we must treat them as if they were pagan. "But now I am writing to you that you must not associate with anyone who claims to be a brother or sister but is sexually immoral or greedy, an idolator or slanderer, a drunkard or swindler. Do not even eat with such people" (1 Corinthians 5:11).

But what if the Church herself abdicates her role? Then what? Does she even know what her role is?

Church elders, please don't use "God will avenge" as your excuse not to fulfill the role of the Church in Matthew 18. Please don't use "they've moved on," shrugging your shoulders at the need to call certain men and women to account as they jump from one sheepfold to the next. The Church is the Church, no matter where the gathering is held. Men in eldership are there to act justly, keep peace, confront sin, and hold other men in leadership accountable.

Elders, I beg you, don't turn a deaf ear and blind eye to what you know is wrongdoing in the house of God! Do not cower in fear to bullying, manipulative tactics coming from those in authority! Involve everyone in open dialogue because all parties need to be heard and represented. Everyone must be held accountable for their words and actions. This is the only way to find out the truth and identify wrongdoing. Don't just take another pastor's word for it regarding someone else. It could be they're covering up what they don't want you to know. Let the other party speak for themselves! Nothing less will do. These pastors do not have the interests of others in mind, only their own appetites!

"Silence in the face of evil is itself evil: God will not

hold us guiltless. Not to speak is to speak. Not to act is to act." –Dietrich Bonhoeffer

How much longer? How much longer until men of pastoral, eldership, or mission board roles STAND UP against these imposters? Do you not recognize them by their fruit, or do you not understand how these deceivers, devourers, and dividers operate? Do you not understand that your silence is your participation in these grievances and horrific acts of injustice within the Church?

Accountability is an absolute *must* in the house of God, or the whole thing will perish from the abuses of these self-appointed men! This is not the time to schmooze your way into another position of power or volley for your next time with the microphone on the platform! It's not about you! It's about God's sheep, the people of his pasture.

> "The word of the Lord came to me: 'Son of man, prophesy against the shepherds of Israel; prophesy and say to them: 'This is what the Sovereign Lord says: Woe to you shepherds of Israel who only take care of yourselves! Should not shepherds take care of the flock? You eat the curds, clothe yourselves with the wool and slaughter the choice animals, but you do not take care of the flock. You have not strengthened the weak or healed the sick or bound up the injured. You have not brought back the strays or searched for the lost. You have ruled them harshly and

brutally. So they were scattered because there was no shepherd, and when they were scattered they became food for all the wild animals. My sheep wandered over all the mountains and on every high hill. They were scattered over the whole earth, and no one searched or looked for them.' 'Therefore, you shepherds, hear the word of the Lord: As surely as I live, declares the Sovereign Lord, because my flock lacks a shepherd and so has been plundered and has become food for all the wild animals, and because my shepherds did not search for my flock but cared for themselves rather than for my flock, therefore, you shepherds, hear the word of the Lord: This is what the Sovereign Lord says: I am against the shepherds and will hold them accountable for my flock. I will remove them from tending the flock so that the shepherds can no longer feed themselves. I will rescue my flock from their mouths, and it will no longer be food for them.'" Ezekiel 34:1-10

CHAPTER 14

"95 MODERN THESES"

I f anyone has the belief that we may be in the "last days," please understand that many hearts have already gone cold and exhibit the characteristics of corrupted men.

"But mark this: There will be terrible times in the last days. People will be lovers of themselves, lovers of money, boastful, proud, abusive, disobedient to their parents, ungrateful, unholy, without love, unforgiving, slanderous, without self-control, brutal, not lovers of the good, treacherous, rash, conceited, lovers of pleasure rather than lovers of God— having a form of godliness but denying its power. Have nothing to do with such people." 2 Timothy 3:1-5

Sometimes the heart becomes so hard, the ears don't just become "hard of hearing," they become deaf. Vision doesn't just become blurry—eyes become completely blind. In this case, that man or woman in their sin (worshipping or serving something other than God and his will) has little chance of survival.

This is when God will speak louder and move in greater ways in order to get someone to hear or see. We can find this example in the Bible when Jesus addresses the Pharisees, or the "religious elite," of his day. Jesus doesn't mince words, and he offends these men when he calls them a "brood of vipers" (Matthew 12:34), and "whitewashed tombs" full of dead bones (Matthew 23:27). From all appearance, these men were godly, righteous leaders who represented the will of God himself to the people.

I believe God has something to say, so listen up, leaders of the Church! Whoever has ears, let them hear.

"95 Modern Theses"

Dear Pastor, or "Religious Elite," of Today:

1. **Stop talking at the people.**
2. Stop your stories, your history lessons, and your entertaining photos and videos.
3. Stop making every Sunday feature *your* teaching lesson.
4. There is no glory in the microphone, amplifying your prowess, skill, and ability for all to hear.
5. How long do you spend crafting a perfect sermon while you neglect to get to know your sheep?

6. Teach everyone to open the scriptures and let the Holy Spirit speak.

7. Each person can bring a word, a scripture, or a song; therefore, divvy out the microphone.

8. Do nothing out of selfish ambition or vain conceit; value others above yourself. (Phil. 2:3)

9. **Your seminary diploma means very little.**

10. We understand you may have spent time and money to study the Word.

11. Do not make seminary a requirement in order to be 'hired' for a pastoral position.

12. The people do not need to be fed by your intellectually 'puffed up knowledge.' (1 Cor. 8:1)

13. It doesn't take a seminary degree to preach the gospel or to qualify one for ministry.

14. Consider how the church is growing in persecuted countries around the world and learn from it.

15. Let God be the judge and selector of church leadership through the guidance of the Holy Spirit.

16. **Discover spiritual gifts.**

17. Stop exercising *your* spiritual gift until you have spent the time to discover *someone else's.*

18. There are others in your congregation that have hidden, dormant gifts that the church needs.

19. Do not build a pride-breeding platform for yourself to display your gifting for all to see.

20. The people need to look to the Holy Spirit to guide, equip, comfort, and counsel them, not you.

21. Discover and utilize everyone else's gifts so *each member does his/her part* (Ro. 12:4-6).

22. **Do not steal the Lord's glory.**
23. Do not promote yourself or your wisdom, and make sure the people are not in awe of you.
24. Your piece of paper that says you studied the Scripture does not qualify you.
25. God will not give his glory to another so give public credit to God alone, and do it often.
26. Do not steal his glory based upon your knowledge, wise, and persuasive words (1 Cor. 2:4).
27. The Holy Spirit has an integral role in the church so make sure you're not replacing him.
28. **Do not take the church's money.**
29. What is your salary and retirement fund from your sheep's tithes and offerings?
30. Do you think your own food, clothing, shelter, and 401K is more important than the lost?
31. Are you clothing the naked, feeding the hungry, and providing the poor wanderer with shelter?
32. Don't pad your pockets with the church's money because you prepared a teaching lesson.
33. Why would the 'average' believer have any desire to serve free of charge if you are getting paid?
34. Please give *more* to help those in *need* than your church consumes within the overall budget.
35. Feed the hungry and the lost before you feed yourself. (John 21:17)
36. Consider tent-making to earn your keep.
37. **Do not establish and teach doctrine based upon your own interpretation of Scripture.**
38. We don't need you to read the Scripture to us; we can read, and the Holy Spirit can interpret.

39. Why would we need to read and study the Word when you do it for us?
40. We don't need you to set up doctrines and twist scripture to match your own beliefs.
41. Do not water down the moral standards of God or the seriousness of sin.
42. Do not over-emphasize "grace" while neglecting truth and giving license for sin. (Jude 1:4)
43. Isn't there enough division within the Christian church's umpteen denominations?
44. What kind of testimony is the severely divided, ununified Christian church giving the world?
45. **Do not focus on numbers.**
46. We don't care how many people are in 'your' church or how many 'followers' you have.
47. Bigger numbers do not equal success just as smaller numbers do not equal failure.
48. Get rid of the territorial or competitive spirit among church gatherings within your community.
49. Focus on UNITY and stop comparing (John 17:23).
50. **Do not use God's money for buildings and capital projects.**
51. We could care less about the size of your budget and your 'amazing' plans for capital projects.
52. We're tired of the church's money going into carpet, technology, parking lots, and buildings.
53. We're not impressed with brick-and-mortar just as Jesus was not impressed with the temple.
54. Get God's heart for the hungry, naked, thirsty, gospel-destitute people headed for hell.

55. We don't need our own comfort or a modern building; we need souls won into the Kingdom.
56. We can gather outside or in homes, breaking bread together and practicing hospitality.
57. **Do not avoid confrontation, blame shift, respond defensively, or make excuses.**
58. If you cannot be challenged or confronted by another believer, why are you in leadership?
59. It's time to exercise Matthew 20:25-28 and stop 'lording over' your people.
60. You're at the 'bottom of the ladder,' so don't cut others down to make yourself feel bigger.
61. Who gave you the right to exercise your authority over the people in your care?
62. The Kingdom of God is an upside-down kingdom.
63. If you want to rule with spiritual authority, congratulations, you just became the least.
64. If you want to be great in God's Kingdom, you must be a humble servant of all.
65. **Disciple your people.**
66. Teach your people to *obey* Jesus' commands in the Great Commission (Matthew 28:19).
67. Send them OUT to work the fields instead of always gathering them IN to consume your gift.
68. Do not try to 'keep' the people dependent on you, or stifle their growth if it challenges you.
69. Focus on the command of Jesus that says, "GO," instead of guiding people to sit in the pews.
70. Evangelism and Discipleship must be taught and regularly practiced by all for multiplication.

71. Let's put as much, if not *more*, time/energy into outreach events as we do inhouse 'programs.'
72. **Return the Power to the People.**
73. Stop gathering hundreds and thousands of people around just a few men who can speak well.
74. You have absolutely no capability of shepherding hundreds or thousands of people.
75. The people have voices, hands, and feet too that God wants to use in order to bring in a harvest.
76. God gives vision and strategy even to 'the common'; it doesn't always need to come from you.
77. *Listen* to your sheep and do the best you can to *steward* God's calling on their lives.
78. We don't care how well-known/revered your name is in the local or virtual Church community.
79. Lifting up a man only sets him up for pride and failure, and when he falls, so do others.
80. Teach the people to look to God alone rather than man, and then their foundation is secure.
81. **Provide a shepherd. (Mark 6:34)**
82. If your teaching is gathering hundreds or thousands of listeners, you must provide shepherds so none are lost.
83. Give a structure to the church where each person is charged with the care of another/others.
84. Each person needs to *be* a shepherd caring for another as well as *be* shepherded by another.
85. Teach the people *how* to shepherd as they practice the "one another" Scriptures.
86. Perhaps the people are looking for a *shepherd*, wandering from one congregation to the next?

87. **Becoming a pastor is not a "career" choice.**

88. You cannot select to be a pastor as others can select secular jobs.

89. Becoming a minister is a calling from the Lord so make sure you're in the right calling.

90. Being a pastor or leader in the church is a responsibility too great to mess up (Luke 17:2).

91. Please step down if you're prone to pride, hidden sin, fear of man, or building yourself up.

92. Please step down if you're unable to confront sin in someone's life (Matthew 18:15-20).

93. Please step down if you're unable to sacrifice your needs for the needs of others.

94. Ministry can be an idol, the American Church can be a business, and the Holy Spirit *grieved*.

95. **The Gospel Must Be Preached!**

"Then the Lord said to him, 'Now then, you Pharisees clean the outside of the cup and dish, but inside you are full of greed and wickedness. You foolish people! Did not the one who made the outside make the inside also? But now as for what is inside you—be generous to the poor, and everything will be clean for you. Woe to you Pharisees, because you give God a tenth of your mint, rue and all other kinds of garden herbs, but you neglect justice and the love of God. You should have practiced the latter without leaving the former undone. Woe to you Pharisees, because you love the most important seats in the synagogues and respectful greetings in the marketplaces. Woe to you, because you are like unmarked graves, which people walk over without knowing it.' One of the experts in the law answered him, 'Teacher, when you say these things, you insult us also.' Jesus replied, 'And you experts in the law, woe to you, because you load people down with burdens they can hardly carry, and you yourselves will not lift one finger to help them. Woe to you, because you build tombs for the prophets, and it was your ancestors who killed them. So you testify that you approve of what your ancestors did; they killed the prophets, and you build their tombs. Because of this, God in his wisdom said, 'I will send them prophets and apostles, some of whom they will kill and others they will persecute.' Therefore this generation will be held responsible for the blood of all the prophets that has been shed since the beginning of the world, from the blood of Abel to the blood of Zechariah, who was killed between the altar and the sanctuary. Yes, I tell you, this generation will be held responsible for it all. Woe to you experts in the law, because you have taken away the key to knowledge.

You yourselves have not entered, and you have hindered those who were entering.'"
Luke 11:39-52

CHAPTER 15

TRUE SPIRITUAL LEADERSHIP

"Sitting down, Jesus called the Twelve and said, 'Anyone who wants to be first must be the very last, and the servant of all." Mark 9:35

I've been involved in various activities in which there was leadership over me. Let me say this: people will let you down. Reviewing each situation—especially this most recent conundrum—has left me longing for the maturity and wisdom of a truly Christlike, humble servant leader. I've compiled a list of character traits that I would have loved to experience from the various mentors in my life that have let me down.

<u>Qualities of the Spiritual Leader I always wanted but never had:</u>

Someone who is willing and able to meet with me weekly or bi-weekly.

Someone who is an excellent listener.

Someone who can put themselves in my shoes.

Someone who does not portray themself as the 'expert' and me as the ignorant, inept 'student.'

Someone who asks clarifying questions to better understand me and draw out my thoughts.

Someone who gives value and weight to my ideas.

Someone who accepts my contribution or offer to help so I feel needed and useful.

Someone who will acknowledge receipt when they receive important communications from me.

Someone who can skillfully manage conflict-resolving discussions.

Someone who can mediate between parties and let everyone be heard.

Someone who has accountability and keeps others accountable.

Someone who will not use me or leech off me to boost their own ego or ministry.

Someone who will teach me to recognize and keep healthy boundaries.

Someone who will clarify roles and expectations in team settings.

Someone who will love me regardless of my performance.

Someone who wants a relationship with me outside of work.

Someone who will empower me and help me grow.

Someone who is faithful in prayer and skilled in spiritual warfare.

Someone who will give me room to exercise my skills and allow me to practice leading.

Someone who is not prone to jealousy.

Someone who will not sabotage my success out of their own insecurity.

Someone who is humble and willing to apologize.

Someone who does not blame or shame me by exploiting my weaknesses in order to get off the hook.

Someone who will not leave me when times get tough.

Someone who always believes the best of me and speaks into who I am as a child of God.

Someone who will encourage me to soar into my potential rather than keep me contained.

Someone who is not focused on keeping the limelight but rather develops the giftings of others.

◆

Does this all sound too difficult? Are these unattainable? Human beings are imperfect. I certainly know I am, but I don't believe this kind of leader is impossible. I think every believer can aim to grow in Christ and exemplify these mature traits. Conclusively, I believe these skills and abilities all stem from one foundational quality: humility.

In contrast, the worldly model and structure of leadership is a "top-down" mentality. This is often referred to as "climbing the ladder" in the corporate world in which the "elite" sit at the very top of the organization. They control and command everything "under" them. Sometimes I wonder if power is intoxicating.

However, the Kingdom of God is an upside-down kingdom where I believe the model of leadership is inverted. In referring to the Church as a metaphorical building, Scripture clearly states that biblical leadership provides a foundation of apostles and prophets with the chief cornerstone as Jesus himself (Ephesians 2:20).

In this picture, the foundation of the Church is located at the very bottom of the structure and serves to support and build everyone else up. This leadership model places those in the charge and keeping of others at the very lowest position, providing support for everything that follows.

Perhaps the most poignant picture of leadership Jesus gave was when he knelt to wash the feet of his disciples (John 13). He physically lowered his body close to the floor in front of the one he was leading. This stunning portrayal of humble servanthood captures the essence of Christlike leadership. He sets the perfect example. This is the example I want to follow and represent to others. This is the example I desire to be exhibited by whomever would steward me.

This type of leader makes no decision and takes no action to suit their own plans and purposes, but rather takes into first consideration the needs of the one they are leading. "Do nothing out of selfish ambition or vain conceit. Rather, in humility value others above yourselves, not looking to your own interests but each of you to the interests of the others" (Philippians 2:3-4). This type of leadership requires placing the needs of others in front of their own. It takes sacrifice. "I am the good shepherd. The good shepherd lays down his life for the sheep" (John 10:11).

I've also sadly come across an "ownership" mentality from those in authority over me. These people provided little room for my thoughts, words, and feelings, but were merely interested in what I could offer or contribute to validate them and their ministry agenda. The mentality of "owning" the flock in one's care is incorrect. Validation should only come from the Lord.

I think shepherds or leaders of the Church need to be very careful not to adopt this kind of thinking. The sheep of their pasture are the Lord's alone. Shepherds are merely to feed their sheep, encourage them into faith, love and good deeds, and act as guardians of protection so that the wolves or other predators do not secretly slip in and devour them.

Unfortunately, I wasn't protected. I was taken advantage of by the "shepherds" surrounding me. I've found myself at the very "bottom" of this worldly, hierarchical structure of power the Church has adopted, as some of you may have also experienced. From this vantage point, I've had time to ponder and have a few more thoughts.

Why do I think any one has any ability, talent, or wisdom of their own to offer the world? People only have what God has given. Why think of someone more important than the rest? I can celebrate other's gifts as a reflection of the glory of God shining through his creation. However, I have to be careful not to elevate or demote people's rankings or status based on worldly ideology. I need to see people as God sees them. People are people. "For by the grace given me I say to every one of you: Do not think of yourself more highly than you ought, but rather think of yourself with sober judgment, in accordance with the faith God has distributed to each of you" (Romans 12:3).

Why should I be jealous of other people's gifts? If I have only 1 talent, but that other person has been given 10, why should I complain? I'd have to take up my argument with God, remembering he does as he pleases. It is simply my duty to please him by faithfully utilizing whatever I have been given. To one he gives 10 talents, to the other 5, and to another only 1 (Matthew 25:14–30).

Who am I to judge others? In the same way, he pays out rewards how he chooses as Jesus taught in the Parable of the Workers in the Vineyard (Matthew 20). I don't need to look sideways at what someone else has been rewarded, and think I deserve just as much if not more. I can let God be the judge and let him make decisions on how he wants to reward his servants. "No servant is greater than his master" (John 13:16).

Why do I think I can accomplish anything without him? Everything lives, moves, and breathes because of him. If Jesus indeed lives inside my heart, the fruit I produce will verify and speak for itself of my faith in Christ and his working through me. "I am the vine; you are the branches. If you remain in me and I in you, you will bear much fruit; apart from me you can do nothing" (John 15:5).

Any man who claims to be wise and raises his head higher than the rest of the grassy field of humanity better watch out for God's lawn mower because he's leveling the field. Those who have raised themselves up apart from God will soon find themselves brought low. It's already happening. "All people are like grass, and all their glory is like the flowers of the field; the grass withers and the flowers fall, but the word of the Lord endures forever" (1 Peter 1:24-25).

Clamoring to glorify oneself or hold one's important position by crushing others or keeping them contained is unnecessary. If the men of the Church are busy squabbling and grappling amongst themselves for who has the "correct" denomination, who will be the greatest, and who will have the biggest budget, best facilities, and brightest teaching, how can the body of Christ function if it's cutting and mutilating itself? "For the wisdom of this world is foolishness in God's sight" (1 Corinthians 3:19).

If the men of the Church are not preaching truth in love or obeying the gospel, even the rocks will cry out! Consequently, the gifts of the Spirit have been given for men and women alike. If the men are competing with each other all the while slandering women, then what other choice does the Lord have than to also raise up women to preach the gospel and make disciples? It's not a gender war, but rather an issue of love. "There is neither Jew nor Gentile, neither slave nor free, nor is there male and female, for you are all one in Christ Jesus" (Galatians 3:28).

God uses men as well as women. God's sons *and daughters* will prophesy in the last days (Joel 2:28). If mission organizations send out single women to preach the gospel, why do others think themselves lofty enough to cut women down? Furthermore, one will find examples of women leaders in the Old Testament as well as examples in recent history who've had the gifts of the Holy Spirit working through them, so why do the men of the Church have to cast condemnation upon women who are serving Christ? Do ministers understand this attitude is belittling, silencing, and disqualifying women from spreading the Word and preaching the gospel? Just do the work of the Church and stop the fruit of slander.

Let's not become prideful in our own thinking. Let's stop belittling each other, arguing over gender, and instead focus on the Church's duties to reach the lost. Everyone is needed. Let's start acting in unity and obedience to the Lord's commands and his Great Commission. Stop cutting others apart in order for you to "ascend" into a seat of importance. That's not the right fruit, so don't find yourself fighting against the Lord. Let the Lord judge people's hearts and choose whomever he wants to use, man or woman.

God desires his children to be made perfect in love. His desire is for his children to know his love, experience his love, and grow into the fullness of the stature and measure of Christ's love. He has given various ministry roles and gifts to men and women, not to compete, but to complement each other while serving the Lord. Only *then* can we lead our brothers and sisters in Christ in absolute honor, integrity, and humility. *Then* the world will know! "By this everyone will know that you are my disciples, if you love one another" (John 13:35).

> "So Christ himself gave the apostles, the prophets, the evangelists, the pastors and teachers, to equip his people for works of service, so that the body of Christ may be built up until we all reach unity in the faith and in the knowledge of the Son of God and become mature, attaining to the whole measure of the fullness of Christ."
> Ephesians 4:11-13

I'd like to point out the different offices of the Church the Lord has appointed in the above passage. Somehow the mainstream American Christian Church today seems to center only around motivational, teaching pastors.

Many claim their own doctrine as sound while canceling others and publicly calling them out as "false teachers." It seems to me mainstream teaching pastors have chased both apostle and prophet out of the Church and its walls. Where else can the prophets go to share the word of the Lord other than online if the pastors and teachers won't accept them? Could it be because they don't really want to hear what God has to say?

It seems to me certain religious teachers spend more time condemning others as "false" and have built a ministry upon proving themselves right and others wrong rather than walking in unity and love, obeying the Great Commission to the praise and glory of the Father. It's a dog-eat-dog world out there in the public eye. The Church body is malfunctioning and cutting itself into thousands of pieces out of pride, selfish ambition, and jealousy. What kind of testimony are we exuding? The world is strife with deception and confusion. Let us be a people who love God and truly love others in unity, giving preference to one another's gifts and lifting each other up. Only then will we shine in the darkness. "This is how we know what love is: Jesus Christ laid down his life for us. And we ought to lay down our lives for our brothers and sisters" (1 John 3:16).

What is love, and where is it? Like me, perhaps you have also felt unloved and unlovable. The people in your life may have left you completely shattered, devalued, and downright hopeless or depressed. The people you looked up to that were meant to stay, to care, to listen, or to love, may not have exemplified these characteristics in your relationship. They may have done the very opposite. But let us not confuse the limited ability of a human being with the perfect Author of Love.

It is very difficult to love others and treat others with love when you have been abused yourself or been led to believe you are worthless by those around you. Or perhaps you've been treated as if you were simply a means to someone else's ends, and when you didn't meet their needs, they discarded you and made you believe you had nothing to offer. If this is you, my heart goes out to you. I know what a struggle this can be for one's identity, value, and worth.

This is why I believe everyone can benefit from a better understanding of God's love. Not only knowledge, but an experience of God's love to erase any shadows of doubt. Might I suggest we all need healing, including myself. We all need a touch from God!

Why have so many people missed God's love? I think one reason is because there's either a staggering absence of human fathers or unhealed "father wounds." I'm one as well whose life has been impacted at times during childhood by a physically present but emotionally absent father. I didn't realize this had left a wound of abandonment in my life. Perhaps you too have been impacted by the plight of fatherlessness.

A few years back my dad and I visited a graveyard in which many of his family members had been buried. He mentioned his grandfather had "closed himself off" after the death of one of his four-year-old twin daughters. In addition, my dad's father served in World War II and was conditioned to be a tough man in order to match the disciplined, army mentality in preparation for war. As a result, these two men had circumstances in their lives that impacted their ability to show emotion and give love to their children.

My dad also walked through the grief recovery book and texted me one day that he had written a forgiveness letter to his dad. I had no idea, but now the dots were connecting. Generational sin is real (Exodus 20:5). This woundedness is still playing out in our family through my estranged, angry younger brother. How easy it is for a person to pass along wounds to the next generation rather than health and wholeness!

Why is this? Why the fathers? I think the severe attack on fathers is a tactic Satan uses to keep children feeling orphaned with a gaping, wounded heart, unable to comprehend or experience the love of a father, especially love from God the Father. The effects of this have impacted every following generation as the identity of an orphan has settled itself comfortably in the hearts of those longing for fulfilling relationships with the father figures in their lives, yet unable to fully make that connection.

It's like we live in a giant world of walking wounded: orphaned and abandoned children who so desperately wanted to have this meaningful relationship or receive this love but were injured instead. Children who are naturally looking for a fulfilling relationship with a human, earthly father (or mother) may find this longing fall short due to any number of circumstances. To draw conclusions regarding one's identity or worth from other imperfect human beings may result in a construed viewpoint.

Might I suggest we haven't really understood God's love, received deep inner healing, or adopted our identity of truly being his son or daughter? One can only find their source of identity and value in relationship with their Creator. This is why we need a fresh encounter with the Father's heart more than ever.

God's love is not based upon one's performance, talents, accomplishments, social status, or net worth. God's love is not dependent upon the way one has been treated by others or by the presence or absence of parents, family, or friends. God's love goes deeper and wider and higher than any mind can fathom or anyone's words can possibly describe. God's love is unconditional. It exists outside of and separate from the circumstances of one's life, whether good or bad.

Aside from all the things that can either satisfy or terrify one's life on this earth, "God is love" (1 John 4:16). This fact is unchangeable and eternal. Our minds struggle to even comprehend eternity! When all else is shaken, stripped away, and completely removed, God is still there, and his love still remains. There's nothing anyone or anything can do—whether physical or spiritual—to destroy the existence of God's love. It is stronger than the grave itself. "Love never fails" (1 Corinthians 13:8).

God's love is powerful and accessible. He moved heaven and earth to reach his creation and rescue them from sin and darkness. Others can try to cancel or reject God's love in unbelief or bitterness at their lot in life, being destroyed by the devil's lies and the futility of man's thinking. No matter what anyone else can think, do, or say, they cannot change the existence of God's love or his extension of grace and salvation through his Son Jesus.

> "For I am convinced that neither death nor life, neither angels nor demons, neither the present nor the future, nor any powers, neither height nor depth, nor anything else in all creation, will be able to separate us from the love of God that is in Christ Jesus our Lord." Romans 8:38-39

CHAPTER 16

REPENTANCE AND REVIVAL

This is my story with leadership in the Christian Church, and I've said what I've wanted to say. If they did these grievous acts to me, they would do it to you. In my opinion, the American Christian Church is more than just a sorry sight. It's a disaster zone in complete disorder and disarray. What can anyone do about it anyway? It's so easy to throw up my hands, sigh in exasperation, and go lay down on the bed again in fatalistic fashion. I've become quite inconsolable with a developed "pastor" complex and an aversion to their establishments.

Many participants wanting to hold onto this 'system' may paint me as the enemy and attack me as such. Been there, done that. Tear me apart if you wish. Refute what I have to say, fine. I'm not perfect either. I'm just sharing my experience and thoughts. You can come to your own conclusions. But might I suggest we ask the Lord to check our own hearts first and foremost (Psalm 139:23-24).

Am I a "divider?" Am I stirring up conflict? Yes, I am. God is rightly dividing and separating sheep from goats. He is winnowing out false shepherds (aka "wolves") from his flocks. He's demoting unfaithful shepherds and appointing the humble because he loves his sheep. The spiritual battle is about to get more intense, and swords are going to clash. Jesus said, "Do you think I came to bring peace on earth? No, I tell you, but division" (Luke 12:51).

So go ahead, you who are prideful! Join in with the rest of the lot! Throw the first stone if you've given up *everything* and moved your family to a foreign country on the other side of the world in order to save a soul. Go ahead, throw the first stone if you've also borne the weight of 'the system' that has been unwelcomingly hurled upon me. Throw the first stone if your blood also cries out from the ground. Throw the first stone if you've also been marred beyond recognition by the hands of the "Church."

Does anyone claim *I'm* prideful? Let me say this: I've been shipwrecked, abandoned, and sabotaged in a foreign Eastern country—fleeing one country for the next with no home. I've been shellshocked, persecuted, misrepresented, abused, silenced, betrayed, exploited, and expelled from missions and ignored and suppressed by the "Church." I've heard all the manipulation, slander, and lies from "pastors" I can take. ENOUGH.

These hierarchical, religious, political actions performed by these self-appointed leaders are destroying lives and leaving their subjects completely ravaged! Don't be deceived. These destructive patterns forced upon the lives of those in "subjection to authority" take years to recover. *Years*. How will the Church ever grow into maturity? God help us!

I can say all this because I've already lost everything!

I've lost my home church and Agency commissioning. I've lost all my supporters, my mission field, and my reputation has been completely destroyed. I've lost my voice, my honor, and my sense of value as a person. I've had to battle spiritually, emotionally, mentally, socially, and physically. I've fought so many destructive thought patterns, incapacitating grief, and utter brokenness.

If I lose whatever relationships I have left or are further persecuted for speaking the truth, so be it. "But whatever were gains to me I now consider loss for the sake of Christ. What is more, I consider everything a loss because of the surpassing worth of knowing Christ Jesus my Lord, for whose sake I have lost all things. I consider them garbage, that I may gain Christ" (Philippians 3:7-8).

I've been crushed by the weight of guilt and shame laid upon me by these men and women of the Church. I've cried over the lack of a wife and mother I've been able to be to my husband and my children these last few years, and I can see the toll it's taken on my family as well. I have no following and no ministry to risk losing, so there's nothing left to lose! There's nowhere further down to go because I've already fallen off the very "bottom" of the ladder!

I've laid my lifeless body in the arms of Jesus and asked him to carry me and be my next breath. I still choose Jesus. He's all I have and all I need. I've made him my firm foundation and hope secured, regardless of what I have suffered for his Name. If I have to "die" again by the hands of angry, sinful men who don't like what I have to say in this book, fine. I have found unconditional love and a true relationship in Jesus. My Anchor—though the storms of hell may rage and the demons scream around me. "Yet what is due me is in the Lord's hand" (Isaiah 49:4).

I don't want to pretend that I'm fully healed or recovered because I'm honestly not. I'm a broken human being prone to sin at times, longing for the return of Christ—perhaps just like you. I still face residual effects from my experience like the challenges of stress management and loud, startling noises. Some days I wonder if someone who has sustained the entirety of this level of assault can ever be wholly restored while living on this earth. Regardless, I can certainly try.

"That is why, for Christ's sake, I delight in weaknesses, in insults, in hardships, in persecutions, in difficulties. For when I am weak, then I am strong" (2 Corinthians 12:10).

But, praise God, I've also gained so much. This 'perfect storm' Satan brought into my life to take me out only made me wiser and stronger. He did absolutely everything he possibly could in his limited power to make me believe I was unloved, rejected, worthless, hopeless, and voiceless. He tried to make me believe the whole world including God himself had abandoned me. All the forces of hell tried to come against the Spirit of the Living God inside me, and they failed! It didn't work! I'm still standing on his Word! We can trust in the name of the Lord God Almighty even amidst persecution and suffering!

> "God is our refuge and strength, an ever-present help in trouble. Therefore we will not fear, though the earth give way and

> the mountains fall into the heart of the
> sea, though its waters roar and foam and
> the mountains quake with their surging"
> (Psalm 46:1-3).

"You, dear children, are from God and have overcome them, because the one who is in you is greater than the one who is in the world" (1 John 4:4).

"And we know that in all things God works for the good of those who love him, who have been called according to his purpose" (Romans 8:28).

Consequently, God has seen these men and women portraying themselves as righteous in the forefront of the church and mission organizations while lying to the Church behind closed doors for their own personal gain. God has heard every slanderous word out of their mouths, seen the motives of their prideful hearts laid bare, and watched their hands swiftly shed innocent blood. Simply put: He is not pleased.

While we know God is compassionate, long-suffering, slow-to-anger, merciful and gracious—the window of opportunity to repent is coming to a close. For these spiritual career politicians have not loved nor feared the Lord, and they have not spoken truth nor loved their neighbor. Judgment is coming to the house of God.

> "For it is time for judgment to begin with
> the family of God; and if it begins with
> us, what will the outcome be for those
> who do not obey the gospel of God?" 1
> Peter 4:17

"It is a dreadful thing to fall into the hands of the living God." Hebrews 10:31

"Do not be deceived: God cannot be mocked. A man reaps what he sows." Galatians 6:7

God desires order in his house. If you are reading this and you yourself have been a faithless, heartless, ruthless "wolf in sheep's clothing," or have compromised by participating in the 'systems' of this world, there may still be time to repent before he will expose your deeds and blow you away with the breath of his mouth. Perhaps time is up, only God knows. "There is nothing concealed that will not be disclosed, or hidden that will not be made known" (Luke 12:2).

Pastors and elders, if you see someone with bad fruit, call them to account. This is no time to appease man and let the wolves continue to run rampant inside the sheep pen. Clean the interior offices of the Church and its organizations! If you are a steward of the sheep of his pasture, you've *got* to see a wolf for what it is and drive it away before he viciously devours another one of the flock! Set aside all self-interest and any love of power, prestige, profit, prowess, praise, and the purse! Repent while there's still time!

The Church is in a state of absolute chaos. Mayday, mayday! Don't participate in this 'system' or you will be held accountable and you will be judged. This 'system' takes no part of the Lord, and it couldn't be further from the truth found in the Word of God.

"Then I heard another voice from heaven say: 'Come out of her, my people,' so that you will not share in her sins, so that you will not receive any of her plagues; for her sins are piled up to heaven, and God has remembered her crimes." Revelation 18:4-5

Head teaching pastors, provide a humble shepherd for each member. Don't make your elder board simply a panel of men to approve your plans. Utilize your elders and create a network, perhaps groups of twelve who each shepherd a group of twelve, etc.

Don't ask your people to lead small groups in their homes if they don't even have a shepherd assigned directly to them. The people desire a relationship with a shepherd. Don't abandon your sheep! Don't let them wander around from pasture to pasture looking for a shepherd.

Don't think hundreds or thousands of people can rely on one or two teaching pastors as their shepherds. The people don't need your Scripture lessons sans relationship. The sheep desire to be shepherded! You will be held to account.

People of God, stop looking for a religious deliverer. Do not replace your relationship with the Lord with another human. Don't be in awe of any man or woman because no one but Jesus gets the credit. When men fail, don't let it shipwreck your faith. Stand your feet upon the Rock alone, feast on God's Word, and make him your sure foundation and anchor in the storm. Nothing else will do if you want your faith to survive.

People of God, stop looking for a political deliverer. That's what the Jews wanted from Jesus in his day. Jesus wasn't into politics, he was all about his Father's business, ushering God's Kingdom into the hearts of men. We're running a spiritual race and fighting spiritual battles. Yes, do your due diligence and vote godly men and women into office, but remember disciples of Jesus have their eyes set on another prize.

Those in God's Kingdom are not living for this world or the things of this world; rather, they are born again into spiritual life to perform God's purposes and will on earth through the power of his Holy Spirit. We're looking to our heavenly home with the very Presence of God and his Son Jesus Christ. For our wrestle is not physical, but spiritual. The Gospel must be preached!

We've finally arrived at our destination. I'd like to take a moment here to peek behind the curtain into the spiritual world and address one of the unclean spirits behind these described atrocities within Christ's Church: Jezebel.

Mentioned in Revelation chapter 2, Jezebel and her evil, destructive forces can no longer be avoided or tolerated. It's an abomination in the heart of the Church that causes complete desolation! Blood of both prophets and priests of the Lord continually cries out from the ground and has reached a critical mass that the cup of God's wrath and justice can no longer ignore! He's seen and heard it all, and He's had enough of the pride, control, manipulation, jealousy, false witness, and assassination from leaders in his house!

Jezebel spirit, you've messed with the wrong person

because the Spirit of God lives inside me and cannot be overcome! "'Not by might nor by power, but by my Spirit,' says the Lord Almighty" (Zechariah 4:6). Your time's up, Jezebel! Game over! God is now resurrecting the army of dead bones of the saints that Jezebel's false prophets and priests have slaughtered. This awakened army is coming back in the spirit and power of Elijah to overthrow the rule of this evil spirit and its minions in high places in order to clean God's house of mixture and usher in the return of the glory of the Lord like this world has never seen. Holy is the Lord!

Do you want to see revival in human hearts and reformation in our day? I can tell you one thing. It wasn't until *I* repented of idolatry in my *own* heart and turned away from the pursuits and love of this world, that I was born again into new spiritual life and personal revival came. Dead to self, alive to Christ! "I have been crucified with Christ and I no longer live, but Christ lives in me. The life I now live in the body, I live by faith in the Son of God, who loved me and gave himself for me" (Galatians 2:20). This is what it means to live "in Christ," Church!

> "I will sprinkle clean water on you, and you will be clean; I will cleanse you from all your impurities and from all your idols." Ezekiel 36:25

> "They will no longer defile themselves with their idols and vile images or with any of their offenses, for I will save them from all their sinful backsliding, and I will

> cleanse them. They will be my people,
> and I will be their God." Ezekiel 37:23

God then drew me into his heart through the beautiful person of Jesus, and I experienced the love and holiness of God and the Presence of his Spirit like I've *never* known before. This catapulted me into passionately loving and serving the Lord, doing the will of the Father. "No one serving as a soldier gets entangled in civilian affairs, but rather tries to please his commanding officer" (2 Timothy 2:4).

This genuine relationship with God is available to all who repent and call upon the name of the Lord Jesus. Spend time with him. Worship him. He is a personal God! He is jealous for your heart! He wants communion with *you*!

Let's be done with religious rituals while our hearts are chasing after other things. Let's be done with passions, lusts, and pursuits of this world. *Repentance* is the key. We must *pray* and call upon the name of the Lord for salvation from the road leading to destruction.

God forgive us. Not one of us can do right. Not for one second are we apart from sin. We need the Lord. All of us! All our deeds are like filthy rags before him (Isaiah 64:6). God help us! Only he can save. Only he can resuscitate what little life is left in the Church. Only he can do it.

God is ready to do this for his people. The time is now. Holy Spirit, come! Do what only you can do. Convict the hearts of men and women alike. Make yourself ready a people. We want to be made ready. Help us grow and mature into purity and the perfect love of God exhibited through our lives.

God *loves* his Bride, and he is jealous for her! God wants a pure and spotless Bride with hearts set only on him. A Bride who has readied herself, matured into the fullness of Christ's love, and whose mission is leaving Church walls, storming the gates of hell, and freeing as many prisoners as possible. It's about loving God above all else, loving people, and winning souls—nothing less.

The things the Church invests its money in speaks volumes about the current heart state of the Church, and some have wandered away from the will and purposes of God and the commands in his Word. Can you feel the grief in the heart of the Father? It's time to come back.

This is the Church! Nothing will stop God's Church. Not even the devil or death itself. Nothing can separate us from the love of God that is in Christ Jesus our Lord! It's time for the next level.

Rise up, sons and daughters of the one true living God! Rise up, men and women of valor! Let the Lord define who you are. The definitions that worldly standards and systems have slapped on you are coming to an end. They are a lie! Step forward into your mature identity, beautiful Church, full of diverse giftings and callings! You represent the Rock of Ages! Come forth, Lazarus! Let your light shine (Isaiah 60)! Let's run the race in such a way as to get the prize (1 Corinthians 9:24-25). Come, Lord Jesus!

Jesus *will* receive the honor and glory he deserves. No matter the cost, He *will* receive to himself his inheritance—his people—blood-bought, purchased, and redeemed: a pure and spotless Bride. Have you given your *life* to Christ? Are you a part of God's Kingdom inheritance? Does he sit on the throne of *your* heart?

Jesus is worthy!

> "Therefore God exalted him to the highest place and gave him the name that is above every name, that at the name of Jesus every knee should bow, in heaven and on earth and under the earth, and every tongue acknowledge that Jesus Christ is Lord, to the glory of God the Father." Philippians 2:9-11

SCRIPTURES

Introduction

"If they still refuse to listen, tell it to the church; and if they refuse to listen even to the church, treat them as you would a pagan or a tax collector." Matthew 18:17

"By their fruit you will recognize them." Matthew 7:16a

"Dear friends, although I was very eager to write to you about the salvation we share, I felt compelled to write and urge you to contend for the faith that was once for all entrusted to God's holy people. For certain individuals whose condemnation was written about long ago have secretly slipped in among you. They are ungodly people, who pervert the grace of our God into a license for immorality and deny Jesus Christ our only Sovereign and Lord." Jude 1:3-4

"For I resolved to know nothing while I was with you except Jesus Christ and him crucified." 1 Corinthians 2:2

"If anyone speaks, they should do so as one who speaks the very words of God." 1 Peter 4:11a

Chapter 3

"We do not want you to be uninformed, brothers and sisters, about the troubles we experienced in the province of Asia. We were under great pressure, far beyond our ability to endure, so that we despaired of life itself. Indeed, we felt we had received the sentence of death. But this happened that we might not rely on ourselves but on God, who raises the dead." 2 Corinthians 1:8-9

Chapter 4

"And everyone who has left houses or brothers or sisters or father or mother or wife or children or fields for my sake will receive a hundred times as much and will inherit eternal life." Matthew 19:29

Chapter 5

"If your brother or sister sins, go and point out their fault, just between the two of you. If they listen to you, you have won them over." Matthew 18:15

Chapter 6

"But if they will not listen, take one or two others along, so that 'every matter may be established by the testimony of two or three witnesses.'" Matthew 18:16

"If it is possible, as far as it depends on you, live at peace with everyone." Romans 12:18

Chapter 8

"If they still refuse to listen, tell it to the church; and if they refuse to listen even to the church, treat them as you would a pagan or a tax collector." Matthew 18:17

Chapter 9

"The Lord is close to the brokenhearted and saves those who are crushed in spirit." Psalms 34:18

"And has made us to be a kingdom and priests to serve his God and Father—to him be glory and power for ever and ever! Amen." Revelation 1:6

"You have made them to be a kingdom and priests to serve our God, and they will reign on the earth." Revelation 5:10

"Yet it was the Lord's will to crush him and cause him to suffer, and though the Lord makes his life an offering for sin, he will see his offspring and prolong his days, and the will of the Lord will prosper in his hand. After he has suffered, he will see the light of life and be satisfied; by his knowledge my righteous servant will justify many, and he will bear their iniquities." Isaiah 53:10-11

"But I tell you, love your enemies and pray for those who persecute you." Matthew 5:44

"For he bore the sin of many, and made intercession for the transgressors." Isaiah 53:12b

"Bear with each other and forgive one another if any of you has a grievance against someone. Forgive as the Lord forgave you." Colossians 3:13

"For if you forgive other people when they sin against you, your heavenly Father will also forgive you. But if you do not forgive others their sins, your Father will not forgive your sins." Matthew 6:14-15

"I praise you because I am fearfully and wonderfully made; your works are wonderful, I know that full well." Psalm 139:14

"The Lord is gracious and compassionate, slow to anger and rich in love." Psalm 145:8

"'Why do you ask me about what is good?' Jesus replied. 'There is only One who is good. If you want to enter life, keep the commandments.'" Matthew 19:17

"Love never fails." 1 Corinthians 13:8

"Be alert and of sober mind. Your enemy the devil prowls around like a roaring lion looking for someone to devour." 1 Peter 5:8

"For our struggle is not against flesh and blood, but against the rulers, against the authorities, against the powers of this dark world and against the spiritual forces of evil in the heavenly realms. Therefore put on the full armor of God, so that when the day of evil comes, you may be able to stand your ground, and after you have done everything, to stand." Ephesians 6:12-13

Chapter 10

"The Lord will fulfill his purpose for me." Psalm 138:8

"My flesh and my heart may fail, but God is the strength of my life and my portion forever." Psalm 73:26

"You intended to harm me, but God intended it for good to accomplish what is now being done, the saving of many lives." Genesis 50:20

Genesis 22 Abraham tested

"Though he slay me, yet will I hope in him." Job 13:15

"As you know, we count as blessed those who have persevered. You have heard of Job's perseverance and have seen what the Lord finally brought about. The Lord is full of compassion and mercy." James 5:11

"He grew up before him like a tender shoot, and like a root out of dry ground. He had no beauty or majesty to attract us to him, nothing in his appearance that we should desire him. He was despised and rejected by mankind, a man of suffering, and familiar with pain. Like one from whom people hide their faces he was despised, and we held him in low esteem." Isaiah 53:2-3

"Greater love has no one than this: to lay down one's life for one's friends." John 15:13

"Jesus said, 'Father, forgive them, for they know not what they are doing.'" Luke 23:34

"And provide for those who grieve in Zion—to bestow on them a crown of beauty instead of ashes, the oil of joy instead of mourning, and a garment of praise instead of a spirit of despair. They will be called oaks of righteousness, a planting of the Lord for the display of his splendor." Isaiah 61:3

"He makes me lie down in green pastures, he leads me beside quiet waters." Psalm 23:2

"Because of the Lord's great love we are not consumed, for his compassions never fail. They are new every morning; great is your faithfulness." Lamentations 3:22-23

"Let perseverance finish its work so that you may be mature and complete, not lacking anything." James 1:4

"For those God foreknew he also predestined to be conformed to the image of his Son, that he might be the firstborn among many brothers and sisters." Romans 8:29

"The apostles left the Sanhedrin, rejoicing because they had been counted worthy of suffering disgrace for the Name." Acts 5:41

"Therefore, since Christ suffered in his body, arm yourselves also with the same attitude, because whoever suffers in the body is done with sin." 1 Peter 4:1

"Do not love the world or anything in the world. If anyone loves the world, love for the Father is not in them." 1 John 2:15

"For the love of money is a root of all kinds of evil. Some people, eager for money, have wandered from the faith and pierced themselves with many griefs." 1 Timothy 6:10

"No discipline seems pleasant at the time, but painful. Later on, however, it produces a harvest of righteousness and peace for those who have been trained by it." Hebrews 12:11

"Praise be to the God and Father of our Lord Jesus Christ! In his great mercy he has given us new birth into a living hope through the resurrection of Jesus Christ from the dead, and into an inheritance that can never perish, spoil or fade. This inheritance is kept in heaven for you, who through faith are shielded by God's power until the coming of the salvation that is ready to be revealed in the last time. In all this you greatly rejoice, though now for a little while you may have had to suffer grief in all kinds of trials. These have come so that the proven genuineness of your faith—of greater worth than gold, which perishes even though refined by fire—may result in praise, glory, and honor when Jesus Christ is revealed." 1 Peter 1:3-7

"My son, do not despise the Lord's discipline, and do not resent his rebuke, because the Lord disciplines those he loves, as a father the son he delights in." Proverbs 3:11-12

"'For my thoughts are not your thoughts, neither are your ways my ways,' declares the Lord." Isaiah 55:8

"Praise be to the God and Father of our Lord Jesus Christ, the Father of compassion and the God of all comfort, who comforts us in all our troubles, so that we can comfort those in any trouble with the comfort we ourselves receive from God." 2 Corinthians 1:3-4

Chapter 12

"If anyone has material possessions and sees a brother or sister in need but has no pity on them, how can the love of God be in that person?" 1 John 3:17

"The hardworking farmer should be the first to receive a share of the crops." 2 Timothy 2:6

"But if we have food and clothing, we will be content with that." 1 Timothy 6:8

"For from time to time those who owned land or houses sold them, brought the money from the sales and put it

at the apostles' feet, and it was distributed to anyone who had need." Acts 4:34

"Your gold and silver are corroded. Their corrosion will testify against you and eat your flesh like fire. You have hoarded wealth in the last days." James 5:3

"All authority in heaven and on earth has been given to me. Therefore go and make disciples of all nations, baptizing them in the name of the Father and of the Son and of the Holy Spirit, and teaching them to obey everything I have commanded you. And surely I am with you always, to the very end of the age." Matthew 28:18-20

"Leave them; they are blind guides. If the blind lead the blind, both will fall into a pit." Matthew 15:14

"As far as it depends on you live at peace with everyone." Romans 12:18

"A time to love and a time to hate, a time for war and a time for peace." Ecclesiastes 3:8

"My people are destroyed from lack of knowledge." Hosea 4:6

"But the things that come out of a person's mouth come from the heart, and these defile them." Matthew 15:18

"Therefore let us move beyond the elementary teachings about Christ and be taken forward to maturity, not laying

again the foundation of repentance from acts that lead to death, and of faith in God, instruction about baptisms, the laying on of hands, the resurrection of the dead, and eternal judgment." Hebrews 6:1-2

"Not everyone who says to me, 'Lord, Lord,' will enter the kingdom of heaven, but only the one who does the will of my Father who is in heaven." Matthew 7:21

"You believe that there is one God. Good! Even the demons believe that—and shudder." James 2:19

"As the body without the spirit is dead, so faith without deeds is dead." James 2:26

"He will punish those who do not know God and do not obey the gospel of our Lord Jesus." 2 Thessalonians 1:8

"This is the verdict: Light has come into the world, but people loved darkness instead of light because their deeds were evil." John 3:19

"The wrath of God is being revealed from heaven against all the godlessness and wickedness of people, who suppress the truth by their wickedness." Romans 1:18

"The Lord disciplines the one he loves, and he chastens everyone he accepts as his son." Hebrews 12:6

"Enter through the narrow gate. For wide is the gate and broad is the road that leads to destruction, and many enter

through it. But small is the gate and narrow the road that leads to life, and only a few find it." Matthew 7:13-14

"But these people blaspheme in matters they do not understand. They are like unreasoning animals, creatures of instinct, born only to be caught and destroyed, and like animals they too will perish." 2 Peter 2:12

"Yet these people slander whatever they do not understand, and the very things they do understand by instinct—as irrational animals do—will destroy them." Jude 1:10

"And so I tell you, every kind of sin and slander can be forgiven, but blasphemy against the Spirit will not be forgiven." Matthew 12:31

"Not lording it over those entrusted to you, but being examples to the flock." 1 Peter 5:3

"How can you say, 'We are wise, for we have the law of the Lord,' when actually the lying pen of the scribes has handled it falsely? The wise will be put to shame; they will be dismayed and trapped. Since they have rejected the word of the Lord, what kind of wisdom do they have? Therefore I will give their wives to other men and their fields to new owners. From the least to the greatest, all are greedy for gain; prophets and priests alike, all practice deceit. They dress the wound of my people as though it were not serious. 'Peace, peace,' they say, when there is no peace. Are they ashamed of their detestable conduct? No, they have no shame at all; they do not even know how to blush. So they will fall among the fallen; they will be brought down when they are punished, says the Lord. Since my people are crushed, I am crushed; I mourn, and horror grips me. Is there no balm in Gilead? Is there no physician there? Why then is there no healing for the wound of my people?" Jeremiah 8:8-12, 21-22

Chapter 13

"There are six things the Lord hates, seven that are detestable to him: haughty eyes, a lying tongue, hands that shed innocent blood, a heart that devises wicked schemes, feet that are quick to rush into evil, a false witness who pours out lies and a person who stirs up conflict in the community." Proverbs 6:16-19

Ezekiel 8 Idolatry in the Temple

"Or do you show contempt for the riches of his kindness, forbearance and patience, not realizing that God's kindness is intended to lead you to repentance?" Romans 2:4

"Everyone who does evil hates the light, and will not come into the light for fear that their deeds will be exposed." John 3:20

"Woe to them! They have taken the way of Cain; they have rushed for profit into Balaam's error; they have been destroyed in Korah's rebellion." Jude 1:11

"In fact, everyone who wants to live a godly life in Christ Jesus will be persecuted, while evildoers and imposters

will go from bad to worse, deceiving and being deceived."
2 Timothy 3:12

"These people are blemishes at your love feasts, eating with you without the slightest qualm—shepherds who feed only themselves. They are clouds without rain, blown along by the wind; autumn trees, without fruit and uprooted—twice dead." Jude 1:12

"If we claim to be without sin, we deceive ourselves and the truth is not in us." 1 John 1:8

"But now I am writing to you that you must not associate with anyone who claims to be a brother or sister but is sexually immoral or greedy, an idolator or slanderer, a drunkard or swindler. Do not even eat with such people."
1 Corinthians 5:11

"The word of the Lord came to me: 'Son of man, prophesy against the shepherds of Israel; prophesy and say to them: 'This is what the Sovereign Lord says: Woe to you shepherds of Israel who only take care of yourselves! Should not shepherds take care of the flock? You eat the curds, clothe yourselves with the wool and slaughter the choice animals, but you do not take care of the flock. You have not strengthened the weak or healed the sick or bound up the injured. You have not brought back the strays or searched for the lost. You have ruled them harshly and brutally. So they were scattered because there was no shepherd, and when they were scattered they became food for all the wild animals. My sheep wandered over all the mountains and on every high hill.

They were scattered over the whole earth, and no one searched or looked for them.' 'Therefore, you shepherds, hear the word of the Lord: As surely as I live, declares the Sovereign Lord, because my flock lacks a shepherd and so has been plundered and has become food for all the wild animals, and because my shepherds did not search for my flock but cared for themselves rather than for my flock, therefore, you shepherds, hear the word of the Lord: This is what the Sovereign Lord says: I am against the shepherds and will hold them accountable for my flock. I will remove them from tending the flock so that the shepherds can no longer feed themselves. I will rescue my flock from their mouths, and it will no longer be food for them.'" Ezekiel 34:1-10

Chapter 14

"But mark this: There will be terrible times in the last days. People will be lovers of themselves, lovers of money, boastful, proud, abusive, disobedient to their parents, ungrateful, unholy, without love, unforgiving, slanderous, without self-control, brutal, not lovers of the good, treacherous, rash, conceited, lovers of pleasure rather than lovers of God—having a form of godliness but denying its power. Have nothing to do with such people." 2 Timothy 3:1-5

"You brood of vipers, how can you who are evil say anything good? For the mouth speaks what the heart is full of." Matthew 12:34

"Woe to you, teachers of the law and Pharisees, you hypocrites! You are like whitewashed tombs, which look beautiful on the outside but on the inside are full of the bones of the dead and everything unclean." Matthew 23:27

"Do nothing out of selfish ambition or vain conceit. Rather, in humility value others above yourselves, not looking to your own interests but each of you to the interests of the others." Phillipians 2:3-4

"But knowledge puffs up while love builds up." 1 Corinthians 8:1b

"For just as each of us has one body with many members, and these members do not all have the same function, so in Christ we, though many, form one body, and each member belongs to all the others. We have different gifts, according to the grace given to each of us." Romans 12:4-6a

"My message and my preaching were not with wise and persuasive words, but with a demonstration of the Spirit's power, so that your faith might not rest on human wisdom, but on God's power." 1 Corinthians 2:4-5

"I in them and you in me—so that they may be brought to complete unity. Then the world will know that you sent me and have loved them even as you have loved me." John 17:23

"Jesus called them together and said, 'You know that the rulers of the Gentiles lord it over them, and their high officials exercise authority over them. Not so with you.

Instead, whoever wants to become great among you must be your servant, and whoever wants to be first must be your slave—just as the Son of Man did not come to be served, but to serve, and to give his life as a ransom for many." Matthew 20:25-28

Matthew 28:18-20 Great Commission

"When Jesus landed and saw a large crowd, he had compassion on them, because they were like sheep without a shepherd. So he began teaching them many things." Mark 6:34

"It would be better for them to be thrown into the sea with a millstone tied around their neck than to cause one of these little ones to stumble." Luke 17:2

Matthew 18:15-20 Resolving conflict in the Church

"Then the Lord said to him, 'Now then, you Pharisees clean the outside of the cup and dish, but inside you are full of greed and wickedness. You foolish people! Did not the one who made the outside make the inside also? But now as for what is inside you—be generous to the poor, and everything will be clean for you. Woe to you Pharisees, because you give God a tenth of your mint, rue and all other kinds of garden herbs, but you neglect justice and the love of God. You should have practiced the latter without leaving the former undone. Woe to you Pharisees, because you love the most important seats in the synagogues and respectful greetings in the marketplaces. Woe to you, because you are like unmarked graves, which people walk over without knowing it.' One of the experts in the law answered him, 'Teacher, when you say these things, you insult us also.' Jesus replied, 'And you experts in the law, woe to you, because you load people down with burdens they can hardly carry, and you yourselves will not lift one finger to help them. Woe to you, because you build tombs for the prophets, and it was your ancestors who killed them. So you testify that you approve of what your ancestors did; they killed the prophets, and you build their tombs. Because of this, God in his wisdom said, 'I will send them prophets and apostles, some of whom they will kill and others they will persecute.' Therefore this generation will be held responsible for the blood of all the prophets that has been shed since the beginning of the world, from the blood of Abel to the blood of Zechariah, who was killed between the altar an the sanctuary. Yes, I tell you, this generation will be held responsible for it all. Woe to you experts in the law, because you have taken away the key to knowledge. You yourselves have not entered, and you have hindered those who were entering.'" Luke 11:39-52

Chapter 15

"Sitting down, Jesus called the Twelve and said, 'Anyone who wants to be first must be the very last, and the servant of all." Mark 9:35

"Consequently, you are no longer foreigners and strangers, but fellow citizens with God's people and also members of his household, built on the foundation of the apostles and prophets, with Christ Jesus himself as the chief cornerstone." Ephesians 2:20

John 13 Washing of the Disciples' Feet

"Do nothing out of selfish ambition or vain conceit. Rather, in humility value others above yourselves, not looking to your own interests but each of you to the interests of the others." Philippians 2:3-4

"I am the good shepherd. The good shepherd lays down his life for the sheep." John 10:11

"For by the grace given me I say to every one of you: Do not think of yourself more highly than you ought, but rather think of yourself with sober judgment, in accordance with the faith God has distributed to each of you." Romans 12:3

Matthew 25:14-30 Parable of the Talents

Matthew 20 Parable of the Workers in the Vineyard

"No servant is greater than his master." John 13:16

"I am the vine; you are the branches. If you remain in me and I in you, you will bear much fruit; apart from me you can do nothing." John 15:5

"All people are like grass, and all their glory is like the flowers of the field; the grass withers and the flowers fall, but the word of the Lord endures forever." 1 Peter 1:24-25

"For the wisdom of this world is foolishness in God's sight." 1 Corinthians 3:19

"There is neither Jew nor Gentile, neither slave nor free, nor is there male and female, for you are all one in Christ Jesus." Galatians 3:28

"And afterward, I will pour out my Spirit on all people. Your sons and daughters will prophesy, your old men will dream dreams, your young men will see visions. Even on my servants, both men and women, I will pour out my Spirit in those days." Joel 2:28-29

"By this everyone will know that you are my disciples, if you love one another." John 13:35

"So Christ himself gave the apostles, the prophets, the evangelists, the pastors and teachers, to equip his people for works of service, so that the body of Christ may be built up until we all reach unity in the faith and in the knowledge of the Son of God and become mature, attaining to the whole measure of the fullness of Christ." Ephesians 4:11-13

"This is how we know what love is: Jesus Christ laid down his life for us. And we ought to lay down our lives for our brothers and sisters." 1 John 3:16

"You shall not bow down to them or worship them; for I, the Lord your God, am a jealous God, punishing the children for the sin of the parents to the third and fourth generation of those who hate me, but showing love to a thousand generations of those who love me and keep my commandments." Exodus 20:5-6

"God is love." 1 John 4:16

"Love never fails." 1 Corinthians 13:8

"For I am convinced that neither death nor life, neither angels nor demons, neither the present nor the future, nor any powers, neither height nor depth, nor anything else in all creation, will be able to separate us from the love of God that is in Christ Jesus our Lord." Romans 8:38-39

Chapter 16

"Search me, God, and know my heart; test me and know my anxious thoughts. See if there is any offensive way in me, and lead me in the way everlasting." Psalm 139:23-24

"Do you think I came to bring peace on earth? No, I tell you, but division." Luke 12:51

"Yet what is due me is in the Lord's hand." Isaiah 49:4

"That is why, for Christ's sake, I delight in weaknesses, in insults, in hardships, in persecutions, in difficulties. For when I am weak, then I am strong." 2 Corinthians 12:10

"God is our refuge and strength, an ever-present help in trouble. Therefore we will not fear, though the earth give way and the mountains fall into the heart of the sea, though its waters roar and foam and the mountains quake with their surging." Psalm 46:1–3

"You, dear children, are from God and have overcome them, because the one who is in you is greater than the one who is in the world." 1 John 4:4

"And we know that in all things God works for the good of those who love him, who have been called according to his purpose." Romans 8:28

"For it is time for judgment to begin with the family of God; and if it begins with us, what will the outcome be for those who do not obey the gospel of God?" 1 Peter 4:17

"It is a dreadful thing to fall into the hands of the living God." Hebrews 10:31

"Do not be deceived: God cannot be mocked. A man reaps what he sows." Galatians 6:7

"There is nothing concealed that will not be disclosed, or hidden that will not be made known." Luke 12:2

"Then I heard another voice from heaven say: 'Come out of her, my people,' so that you will not share in her sins, so that you will not receive any of her plagues; for her sins are piled up to heaven, and God has remembered her crimes." Revelation 18:4–5

"'Not by might nor by power, but by my Spirit,' says the Lord Almighty." Zechariah 4:6

"I have been crucified with Christ and I no longer live, but Christ lives in me. The life I now live in the body, I live by faith in the Son of God, who loved me and gave himself for me." Galatians 2:20

"I will sprinkle clean water on you, and you will be clean; I will cleanse you from all your impurities and from all your idols." Ezekiel 36:25

"They will no longer defile themselves with their idols and vile images or with any of their offenses, for I will save them from all their sinful backsliding, and I will cleanse them. They will be my people, and I will be their God." Ezekiel 37:23

"No one serving as a soldier gets entangled in civilian affairs, but rather tries to please his commanding officer." 2 Timothy 2:4

"All of us have become like one who is unclean, and all our righteous acts are like filthy rags; we all shrivel up like a leaf, and like the wind our sins sweep us away." Isaiah 64:6

"Arise, shine, for your light has come, and the glory of the Lord rises upon you. See, darkness covers the earth and thick darkness is over the peoples, but the Lord rises upon you and his glory appears over you." Isaiah 60:1-2

"Do you not know that in a race all the runners run, but only one gets the prize? Run in such a way as to get the prize. Everyone who competes in the games goes into strict training. They do it to get a crown that will not last, but we do it to get a crown that will last forever." 1 Corinthians 9:24-25

"Therefore God exalted him to the highest place and gave him the name that is above every name, that at the name of Jesus every knee should bow, in heaven and on earth and under the earth, and every tongue acknowledge that Jesus Christ is Lord, to the glory of God the Father." Philippians 2:9-11

ABOUT THE AUTHOR

Claire lives with her husband Chad and three wonderful children. She enjoys music, coffee, friends, family, and getting out into the beauty of God's creation through hiking, biking, or paddleboarding.

Claire desires to see God's Kingdom rule in the hearts and lives of people as they choose to make Jesus Christ Lord of their life. She also wants to see wounded hearts healed and those who have suffered abuse made whole as God works patiently and gently to restore identity through the power of his love.

She wants the world to know the good news and saving power of Jesus Christ and his coming Kingdom. She is invested in reaching the lives of poverty-stricken, gospel-destitute people in Asia with the good news of Christ through strategic on-the-ground partnerships.